Certification Study Companion Series

The Apress Certification Study Companion Series offers guidance and hands-on practice to support technical and business professionals who are studying for an exam in the pursuit of an industry certification. Professionals worldwide seek to achieve certifications in order to advance in a career role, reinforce knowledge in a specific discipline, or to apply for or change jobs. This series focuses on the most widely taken certification exams in a given field. It is designed to be user friendly, tracking to topics as they appear in a given exam and work alongside other certification material as professionals prepare for their exam.

More information about this series at `https://link.springer.com/bookseries/17100`.

CompTIA Network+ (N10-009) Certification Companion

Hands-on Preparation and Practice Guide

Kodi A. Cochran

Apress®

CompTIA Network+ (N10-009) Certification Companion: Hands-on Preparation and Practice Guide

Kodi A. Cochran
Poca, WV, USA

ISBN-13 (pbk): 979-8-8688-2340-4   ISBN-13 (electronic): 979-8-8688-2341-1
https://doi.org/10.1007/979-8-8688-2341-1

Managing Director, Apress Media LLC: Welmoed Spahr
Acquisitions Editor: Susan McDermott
Project Manager: Jessica Vakili

Cover designed by eStudioCalamar

Distributed to the book trade worldwide by Springer Science+Business Media New York, 1 New York Plaza, New York, NY 10004. Phone 1-800-SPRINGER, fax (201) 348-4505, e-mail orders-ny@springer-sbm.com, or visit www.springeronline.com. Apress Media, LLC is a Delaware LLC and the sole member (owner) is Springer Science + Business Media Finance Inc (SSBM Finance Inc). SSBM Finance Inc is a **Delaware** corporation.

For information on translations, please e-mail booktranslations@springernature.com; for reprint, paperback, or audio rights, please e-mail bookpermissions@springernature.com.

Apress titles may be purchased in bulk for academic, corporate, or promotional use. eBook versions and licenses are also available for most titles. For more information, reference our Print and eBook Bulk Sales web page at http://www.apress.com/bulk-sales.

Any source code or other supplementary material referenced by the author in this book is available to readers on GitHub. For more detailed information, please visit https://www.apress.com/gp/services/source-code.

If disposing of this product, please recycle the paper

Table of Contents

Chapter 4: Network Operations 51

About the Author

Kodi A. Cochran is highly invested in the field of cybersecurity, something he has followed as a hobbyist for the past decade and expanded to make it his field of study and work. He has a bachelor's and master's in Cybersecurity and Information Assurance, in addition to working as an Information Systems Manager for the Networking and Infrastructure team of the Department of Human and Health Resources under the agency of the Office of Management of Information Services at the state of West Virginia.

He's responsible for networking administration, project management, system support, and site support for the state of West Virginia in all state-owned healthcare facilities, hospitals, and labs. In addition, Kodi holds the following certifications: CompTIA A+, Network+, Security+, Project+, CySA+, and Pentest+. He's currently working on the CompTIA CASP+.

About the Technical Reviewer

Md Julfiker Ali Jewel is a software programmer at the West Virginia Department of Health and Human Resources (WV DHHR), where he focuses on secure software development, mainframe modernization, and cybersecurity applications in public sector infrastructure. He holds a master's degree in Computer Science from West Virginia State University, where he also served as a Graduate Research Assistant working on cybersecurity challenges in critical infrastructure protection. Jewel has authored multiple peer-reviewed research papers in artificial intelligence, network security, and public health technology. As an active member of IEEE, ACM, and ISC2, he contributes to technical communities through peer reviews, academic mentorship, and applied AI research. He brings industry experience and academic rigor to his role as a technical reviewer.

CHAPTER 1

Introduction to Networking and the Network+ Certification

Imagine a world without reliable communication: no instant messaging, no video conferencing, no secure banking. Behind every seamless digital transaction lies a sophisticated web of interconnected systems and professionals who design, secure, and manage them. These systems are made of a complex array of devices, all working together for a singular purpose. From routers and switches that act to manage the traffic and aid in actual communication directly, to the firewalls that protect us from unwanted traffic, these devices work together to ensure a seamless experience in our digital world. Consider the airline service outages that made headlines in 2021, when a major technology disruption impacted multiple carriers—grounded flights, stranded passengers, and millions in losses. Such events underscore how critical robust networking is to daily operations across industries.

Today's digital infrastructure is driven by the principles of computer networking. From routine emails and file transfers to highly secure VPN connections and global e-commerce, networking technology is the foundation that supports nearly every interaction in our modern,

© Kodi A. Cochran 2026
K. A. Cochran, *CompTIA Network+ (N10-009) Certification Companion,*
Certification Study Companion Series, https://doi.org/10.1007/979-8-8688-2341-1_1

connected world. These systems are not self-sustaining; they require trained professional network engineers, administrators, and support specialists who possess a deep understanding of protocols, devices, and architecture to keep them operational, secure, and efficient.

The CompTIA Network+ certification and N10-009 exam remain a foundational credential within the IT industry. Recognized globally, this vendor-neutral certification verifies your ability to design, implement, manage, and troubleshoot both wired and wireless networks. It affirms a comprehensive grasp of networking essentials, including device configuration, cabling standards, routing and switching protocols, network security practices, and emerging technologies like cloud computing and virtualization.

Holding this book is your first step in preparing for that professional milestone. The chapters ahead are structured to guide you through core concepts with precision and depth. You'll engage with real-world examples, review exam-relevant material, and develop a framework for not just passing the certification exam but also applying these principles in dynamic workplace environments.

Let's begin your transition from networking student to certified professional.

Understanding the Network+ Certification

The CompTIA Network+ (N10-009) certification represents a comprehensive, vendor-agnostic benchmark for validating the networking proficiency of IT professionals. It encompasses not only the ability to install and configure network hardware but also the expertise to troubleshoot and secure complex network infrastructures across a variety of platforms.

Unlike proprietary certifications that focus narrowly on one vendor's technology stack, Network+ is broad in scope. It allows you to demonstrate transferable, real-world skills applicable in heterogeneous environments—an increasingly important distinction in organizations that rely on a mix of vendors, platforms, and cloud services. In practice, that means being comfortable moving between Windows Server tools, Linux command-line utilities, network operating systems like Cisco IOS/IOS-XE, and cloud consoles. Many organizations are also hybrid by default—an on-prem network extended into an AWS VPC or Azure VNet through a site-to-site IPsec VPN or private connectivity.

Before diving into specific competencies, it's important to understand that Network+ targets both conceptual knowledge and practical application. Each domain in the exam is designed to reflect common, real-world tasks that IT professionals encounter in small, medium, and enterprise-scale environments.

At a high level, the N10-009 exam objectives are grouped into five domains:

- Networking Concepts

- Network Implementation

- Network Operations

- Network Security

- Network Troubleshooting

Behind every seamless digital transaction lies a sophisticated web of interconnected systems and professionals who design, secure, and manage them. These systems are made of a complex array of devices, all working together for a singular purpose. From routers and switches that act to manage the traffic and aid in actual communication directly, to the firewalls that protect us from unwanted traffic. These devices work together to ensure a seamless experience in our digital world. Consider a major airline outage caused by a network misconfiguration—grounded flights, stranded passengers, and millions in losses. Such events underscore how critical robust networking is to daily operations across industries.

Certification is only part of the equation. Reinforce your knowledge through hands-on experimentation. Use simulation tools and lab environments to emulate real networking scenarios.

Core Competencies You Will Develop

- Designing and implementing functional network architecture

- Deploying wired and wireless connectivity using industry standards

- Managing network hardware such as switches, routers, and access points

- Understanding and applying subnetting, VLANs, and IP addressing schemes

- Working with WAN technologies such as MPLS and site-to-site VPNs (IPsec)

- Monitoring and troubleshooting network performance issues

- Securing networks through appropriate protocols and access controls

- Supporting virtualization and cloud-based network solutions

Network+ is strategically positioned between entry-level support certifications such as CompTIA A+ and more specialized credentials like Cisco's CCNA. It's the ideal step for anyone transitioning from general IT support into network engineering, architecture, or security.

Career Opportunities with Network+

The Network+ certification serves as a gateway to a range of career paths in IT. Whether you are starting out or transitioning from a general IT support role, this credential signals to employers that you possess essential, practical networking skills.

Job opportunities span across sectors and organization sizes—from local businesses managing basic LAN environments to global corporations handling advanced wide area networks (WANs). These roles vary in complexity but all require the ability to ensure secure, reliable, and efficient network operations.

Common Roles Include

- **Network Administrator:** Responsible for managing daily operations, security, and efficiency of network infrastructure

- **Systems Administrator:** Oversees servers and networked systems, including file and directory services

- **Network Support Specialist:** Troubleshoots user connectivity issues and ensures reliable network performance

- **IT Field Technician:** Installs and services network hardware onsite

- **Technical Support Specialist**: Provides remote or in-person support for connectivity, access, and performance problems

- **Help Desk Analyst**: Assists users with troubleshooting, typically at Tier 1 or Tier 2 levels

- **Network Analyst**: Analyzes and optimizes existing network configurations and architecture

In addition to expanding job opportunities, Network+ can strengthen your résumé and support salary negotiations, especially when paired with hands-on experience. Salary ranges vary widely by region and role, so use sources like the US Bureau of Labor Statistics and reputable salary aggregators to sanity-check expectations in your market.

Exam Tip #1

Certification is only part of the equation. Reinforce your knowledge through hands-on experimentation. Use simulation tools and lab environments to emulate real networking scenarios. A strong baseline lab is simple but realistic: create a small subnet, stand up DHCP, verify leases from both Windows and Linux, segment traffic with a VLAN, and then troubleshoot when a host can't reach the default gateway. Those small drills build the exact instincts the exam rewards.

How to Use This Book

Success in earning your Network+ certification depends not only on content mastery but also on how well you navigate and engage with your study materials. This book has been carefully structured to align CompTIA's exam objectives while also building your professional competence step-by-step.

Each chapter follows a logical progression that mirrors how networking knowledge is best absorbed—from foundational theory to hands-on application. Whether you are studying independently or in a classroom environment, this book is meant to be your comprehensive guide.

Here's what you'll find in every chapter:

- **Topic Overview**: Provides a summary of what you'll learn and why it matters

- **Detailed Explanations**: Covers technologies, protocols, tools, and scenarios in depth

- **Real-World Context**: Applies concepts to actual environments and enterprise use cases

- **Visual Diagrams**: Enhances retention by illustrating configurations, models, and flow

- **Knowledge Checks**: Includes callouts and mini-assessments to verify understanding

- **Exam Preparation Tips**: Identifies high-yield concepts and common test pitfalls

- **End-of-Chapter Review**: Offers a concise summary and checklist for exam readiness

Before beginning a new chapter, scan its major headings and diagrams. Understanding the structure of the material ahead helps create a mental map, making the content easier to absorb and recall.

Recommended Study Practices

Mastering networking concepts and passing the Network+ exam requires more than just reading—active learning and consistency are key. You'll retain information better and build stronger problem-solving skills by using multiple study methods and engaging with the material in hands-on ways.

This section outlines tried-and-true approaches used by successful certification candidates. By building a daily study habit, reinforcing concepts with tools, and evaluating your progress often, you'll move confidently toward your certification goals.

Effective Study Strategies Include

- **Consistent Daily Study**: Allocate regular time blocks instead of cramming.

- **Lab-Based Practice**: Use simulators like Cisco Packet Tracer, GNS3, or CompTIA CertMaster Labs—or physical labs—to reinforce concepts.

- **Flashcards and Apps**: Leverage tools like Quizlet to review port numbers, protocols, and acronyms.

- **Group Study or Tutoring**: Collaborate with peers or instructors to challenge assumptions and fill gaps.

- **Teach It Aloud**: Teaching a topic, even to yourself, builds neural pathways that strengthen memory.

- **Track Progress**: Maintain a lot of completed objectives and areas needing review.

Exam Tip #2

Take practice exams under timed conditions. Focus not only on right answers, but also on why incorrect choices are wrong. This sharpens both your recall and critical thinking.

Certification Path Overview (Visual)

Refer to Figure 1-1 for a visual summary of the recommended certification pathway. This visual illustrates the progression from entry-level support to advanced networking and security certifications. Network+ serves as a crucial stepping stone that connects foundational knowledge to future specialties in cloud, cybersecurity, and systems architecture.

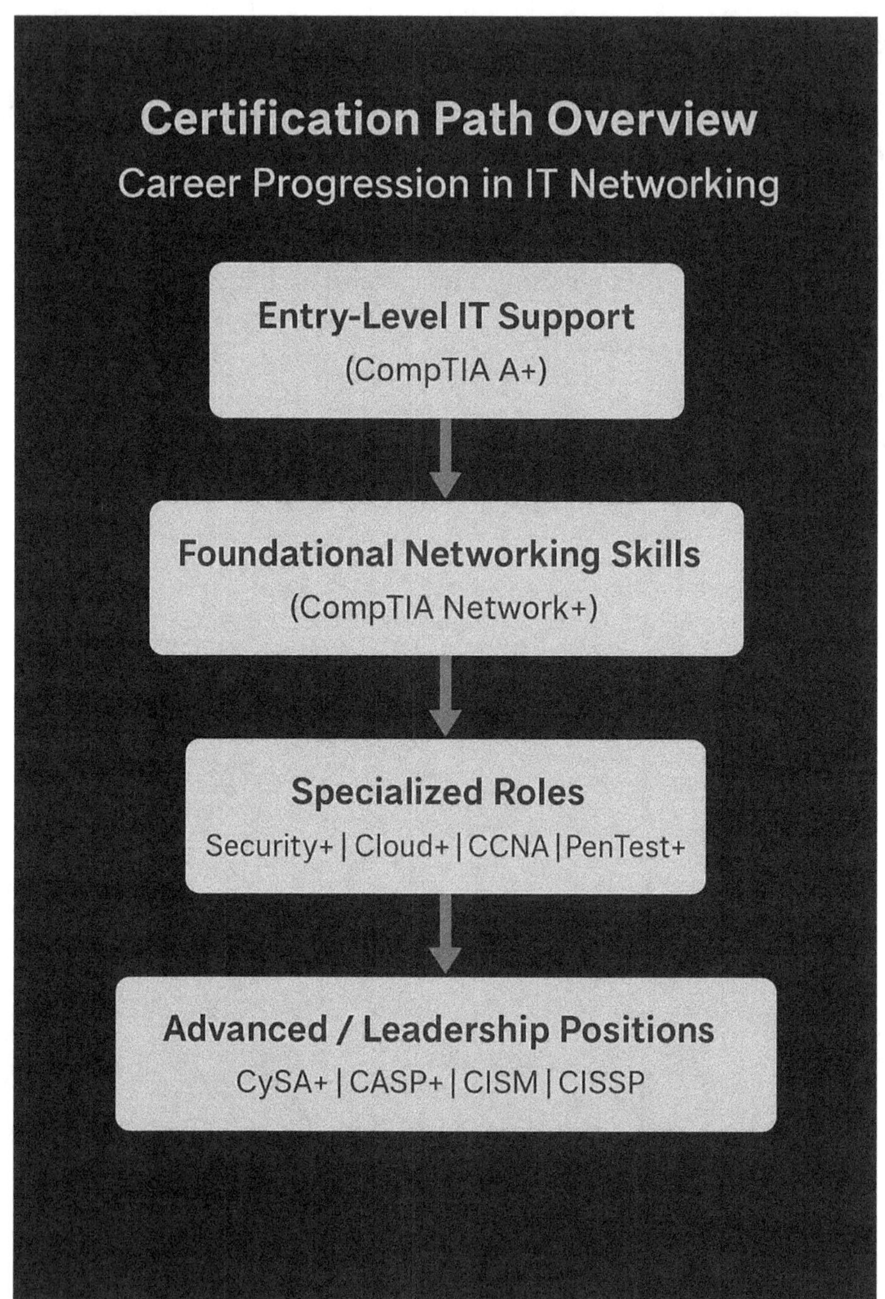

Figure 1-1. *Career progression pathway for IT networking professionals (see Chapter 1)*

The Road Ahead

Now that you understand what the Network+ certification entails and how this book is structured, it's time to set your expectations for the journey ahead. Networking is a vast field, and the material may seem challenging at first—but with persistence, it becomes second nature. Each chapter will build upon the last, introducing new technologies, reinforcing previous topics, and connecting concepts into a larger, integrated understanding of modern networking. By progressing through this sequentially, you'll gain the ability to not only pass the exam but to think like a network technician.

This book is more than a study guide—it's a resource for cultivating a mindset of troubleshooting, continual learning, and infrastructure awareness. From understanding port numbers and cable types to exploring dynamic routing, subnetting, and virtualization, your knowledge will expand with every section. As you move forward, remember to take notes, revisit difficult topics, apply your knowledge in labs or simulations, and stay curious. Network+ isn't just about a credential—it's about preparing to be a capable, confident, and essential contributor to any IT environment.

CHAPTER 2

Networking Fundamentals

In a hyperconnected world, networks are the digital backbone of modern communication, commerce, healthcare, transportation, and beyond. Whether you're streaming a video, backing up data to the cloud, accessing a website, or logging in remotely to a corporate system, your actions depend on a series of precise, invisible network interactions occurring in real time.

This chapter forms the foundational core upon which your networking knowledge will be built. We will begin by exploring the physical and logical components that make up a network, before diving into conceptual models like OSI and TCP/IP that help organize and explain these components. You'll gain a solid understanding of the protocols that govern communication, how devices are addressed, and the structure of IP addressing schemes that make networking possible on a scale.

Mastery of these fundamental ideas is not only essential for passing the CompTIA Network+ exam but also for becoming a capable professional who can think critically and troubleshoot confidently in real-world scenarios.

Let's build the foundation together.

© Kodi A. Cochran 2026

K. A. Cochran, *CompTIA Network+ (N10-009) Certification Companion,*
Certification Study Companion Series, https://doi.org/10.1007/979-8-8688-2341-1_2

Understanding Network Components

Every network is built from a set of physical and virtual devices that serve distinct purposes. These devices—known as network components—form the infrastructure required for systems and users to communicate effectively. To become a proficient networking professional, you need to understand not only what these devices do but how they interact within a larger architecture.

Network components operate at different layers of the OSI model and come in various forms, depending on the network's size, purpose, and complexity. From end user devices to specialized security appliances, knowing their functions is key to diagnosing issues and optimizing performance.

Key Network Components

- **Nodes**: These are any devices capable of sending, receiving, or forwarding data across a network. Common examples include computers, servers, smartphones, and printers. Nodes can be hosts (end devices) or intermediaries like routers and switches. In modern environments, nodes also include IoT devices such as smart cameras, thermostats, smart locks, and environmental sensors.

- **Switches**: Operating at Layer 2 (Data Link Layer), switches connect devices within a Local Area Network (LAN). They use Media Access Control (MAC) addresses to forward data frames to the correct destination. Managed switches provide advanced features like VLANs and port mirroring for diagnostics.

- **Routers**: Functioning at Layer 3 (Network Layer), routers connect different networks and determine the best path for data packets to travel between them. They use IP addresses and routing tables to make forwarding decisions. Routers often include NAT, DHCP, and firewall features.

- **Access Points (APs)**: These provide wireless connectivity by allowing Wi-Fi-enabled devices to connect to a wired network. APs extend coverage, support multiple clients, and can operate as stand-alone units or be controller-managed in enterprise settings.

- **Modems**: Short for "modulator-demodulator," modems convert digital data from a computer into analog signals for transmission over phone lines, DSL, or cable systems—and vice versa. They are often integrated with routers in home networks.

- **Firewalls**: These can be hardware appliances or software applications designed to monitor, permit, or block traffic based on predefined security rules. Firewalls create a barrier between trusted internal networks and untrusted external systems. A host-based firewall (e.g., Windows Defender Firewall) protects a single endpoint, while a network firewall (such as pfSense or a FortiGate appliance) enforces policy between networks for many devices at once.

- **Cables and Connectors**: These include twisted-pair copper cables (like Cat 5e/6), coaxial cables, and fiber-optic lines. Connectors such as RJ-45 and LC/SC interface with devices to carry signals across the network. Common copper categories include Cat 5e, Cat 6, and Cat 6a (and you may also see Cat 7 in some environments). Fiber runs are typically single-mode or multimode, depending on distance and bandwidth requirements.

Exam Tip #3

Switches operate at Layer 2 (Data Link Layer) and route traffic using MAC addresses, while routers operate at Layer 3 (Network Layer) and route traffic based on IP addresses. This distinction is frequently tested on the Network+ exam.

Networking Models: OSI and TCP/IP

To understand how network communication works, it's important to view it through the lens of standardized models. These models provide a consistent framework that describes how data moves between devices and how networking tasks are organized into layers. The two primary models you'll encounter are the OSI Model and the TCP/IP Model. In day-to-day networking, TCP/IP is the de facto model used in practice (and is sometimes referred to as the DoD model), while OSI is primarily a teaching and troubleshooting framework.

These models are foundational because they clarify where different technologies, protocols, and devices operate in the networking stack. Whether you're analyzing a network issue, configuring a switch, or troubleshooting data flow, understanding these models helps you isolate the layer where a problem exists. To understand how network communication works, it's important to view it through the lens of standardized models. These models provide a consistent framework that describes how data moves between devices and how networking tasks are organized into layers. The two primary models you'll encounter are the OSI Model and the TCP/IP Model.

The OSI Model (Open Systems Interconnection)

The OSI Model, developed by the International Organization for Standardization (ISO), divides the networking process into seven distinct layers. Each layer is responsible for specific functions, and each builds upon the capabilities of the layer below it.

The Seven Layers of the OSI Model:

- **Application Layer**: Provides services directly to end users, such as email and file transfers

- **Presentation Layer**: Translates data formats, encrypts, and compresses information

- **Session Layer**: Manages sessions and controls dialogues between devices

- **Transport Layer**: Ensures reliable data delivery, using flow control and error correction (e.g., TCP)

- **Network Layer**: Handles logical addressing and path determination (e.g., IP addressing and routing)

- **Data Link Layer**: Facilitates node-to-node data transfer and manages MAC addressing and frame error detection

- **Physical Layer**: Transmits raw bits over a physical medium (e.g., cables, radio signals)

Memorizing: "Please Do Not Throw Sausage Pizza Away."

Exam Tip #4

Be prepared to identify which OSI layer corresponds to a specific device, protocol, or process. This is a common focus on the Network+ exam.

The TCP/IP Model

The TCP/IP Model is the practical, real-world foundation for modern Internet communication. Unlike the OSI Model, which is primarily conceptual, the TCP/IP Model maps directly to the protocols and operations used in live networks.

It simplifies communication into four layers, each encompassing several OSI functions.

The Four Layers of the TCP/IP Model:

- **Application Layer**: Corresponds to OSI's Application, Presentation, and Session layers; includes protocols like HTTP, SMTP, and DNS

- **Transport Layer**: Manages end-to-end communication, reliability, and data integrity (e.g., TCP, UDP)

- **Internet Layer**: Deals with logical addressing and routing across networks (e.g., IP)

- **Network Access Layer**: Covers physical transmission and protocols like Ethernet and Wi-Fi

Exam Tip #5

Understand that most real-world networks follow the TCP/IP model in practice, even though the OSI model is more commonly used for teaching and troubleshooting.

Common Networking Protocols and Ports

Communication on a network relies on standardized protocol sets of rules that define how data is transmitted between devices. Each protocol typically operates on a specific port number, which acts as a logical endpoint for network services. Together, protocols and ports form the basis of digital communication and are essential for security, troubleshooting, and configuration.

Understanding these associations is crucial for identifying services, setting up firewalls, and responding to alerts. Many questions on the Network+ exam test your ability to recognize which protocol uses which port—and how they apply in real scenarios.

Key Protocols and Their Common Ports:

- **HTTP (Port 80)**: Transfers web pages in plain text over the Internet. It is commonly used for browsing non-secure websites.

- **HTTPS (Port 443)**: Secures web traffic using SSL/TLS encryption, ensuring data privacy and integrity.

- **FTP (Port 21)**: Used for transferring files between client and server systems. Requires authentication.

- **SSH (Port 22)**: Provides secure remote access to network devices and servers via encrypted command-line sessions.

- **DNS (Port 53)**: Resolves domain names (e.g., `www.example.com`) into IP addresses so computers can locate each other.

- **DHCP (Ports 67/68)**: Dynamically assigns IP addresses to client devices, reducing manual configuration.

- **SNMP (Ports 161/162)**: Allows monitoring and management of network devices such as switches and routers. Used in network management systems (NMS).

Exam Tip #6

Focus on memorizing these critical ports and their corresponding protocols. Expect exam questions that match a protocol to its standard port number or ask which port needs to be open for a service to function properly.

Basic IP Addressing: IPv4 and IPv6

Every device connected to a network must have a unique identifier, known as an IP address, to send and receive data accurately. IP addressing is a core concept in networking, used not just for basic connectivity but also for routing, security, and subnetting. There are two primary versions in use today: IPv4 and IPv6. At a high level, MAC addresses identify a network interface at Layer 2 within a local segment, while IP addresses identify a host at Layer 3 so traffic can be routed between networks.

Understanding how these address formats work, how they are structured, and how they differ is critical for both day-to-day network operations and success on the Network+ exam. Every device connected to a network must have a unique identifier, known as an IP address, to send and receive data accurately. IP addressing is a core concept in networking, used not just for basic connectivity but also for routing, security, and subnetting. There are two primary versions in use today: IPv4 and IPv6.

Originally, IPv4 addresses were divided into classes (A, B, C, D, and E), but today Classless Inter-Domain Routing (CIDR) is used for more efficient allocation. CIDR notation includes a suffix (e.g., /24) to denote the subnet mask. IPv6 supports features like stateless address autoconfiguration (SLAAC), simplified header structure, and built-in IPsec for encryption and authentication.

IPv4 Addressing

IPv4 (Internet Protocol version 4) is the most widely used addressing scheme in traditional networks. It provides a 32-bit address space, which is divided into four octets (or bytes). These are typically represented in decimal form, separated by periods.

Example IPv4 Address: 192.168.1.1

1. Each octet can range from 0 to 255.

2. Provides approximately 4.3 billion unique addresses globally.

3. Commonly represented in dotted-decimal format.

Originally, IPv4 addresses were divided into classes (A, B, C, D, and E), but today Classless Inter-Domain Routing (CIDR) is used for more efficient allocation. CIDR notation includes a suffix (e.g., /24) to denote the subnet mask. Classful addressing is largely historical; CIDR is the modern standard, but classful terminology still appears in legacy documentation and on exams. IPv4 also supports private address ranges (e.g., 192.168.x.x, 10.x.x.x) that are commonly used within local networks and are not routable on the public Internet.

IPv6 Addressing

IPv6 (Internet Protocol version 6) was developed to overcome the exhaustion of IPv4 addresses and to improve routing and security.

1. **Address size**: 128 bits

2. **Format**: Eight groups of four hexadecimal digits, separated by colons

3. **Example**: 2001:0db8:85a3:0000:0000:8a2e: 0370:7334

4. **Compressed form**: Zeroes can be abbreviated using: (e.g., 2001: ddb8:)

5. **Address space**: Virtually unlimited—approximately 3.4 x 10^38 addresses

IPv6 supports features like stateless address autoconfiguration (SLAAC), simplified header structure, and built-in IPsec for encryption and authentication. SLAAC relies on ICMPv6 Router Advertisements to learn the network prefix and default gateway, and it can be used by itself or alongside DHCPv6 (e.g., DHCPv6 for additional options) depending on how the network is designed.

Example IPv6 Address: 2001:0db8:85a3:0000:0000:8a2e: 0370:7334

1. Written in hexadecimal and separated by colons

2. Designed to simplify routing and improve security

3. Supports automatic address configuration and efficient packet processing

Exam Tip #7

Know the structural differences between IPv4 and IPv6 and be able to recognize them quickly. Expect exam questions that ask you to distinguish between address types or calculate address ranges.

Firewalls: These can be hardware appliances or software applications designed to monitor, permit, or block traffic based on predefined security rules. Firewalls create a barrier between trusted internal networks and untrusted external systems.

Chapter Summary

In this chapter, you laid the groundwork for your networking education by examining the key components and principles that support all modern networks. You began with a deep dive into the physical devices that drive connectivity—such as switches, routers, access points, and firewalls—building a mental blueprint of how data flows across local and wide area networks.

You then explored two foundational models, the OSI Model and the TCP/IP Model, which structure how data moves between systems. These models not only clarify the networking process but also offer powerful diagnostic frameworks that help you pinpoint issues across the stack.

From there, you moved into real-world implementation details by reviewing essential networking protocols and their corresponding port numbers. These are not just trivia for the exam, they're the heartbeat of every online service, from web browsing to file transfers to device monitoring.

Finally, you tackled one of the most essential concepts in networking: IP addressing. You learned to differentiate between IPv4 and IPv6, understand their formatting and use cases, and apply CIDR notation for subnetting. These skills are critical for configuring networks, managing access, and planning for future scalability. By mastering these core topics, you are now equipped to move forward with confidence. The principles introduced here will appear again and again throughout your studies—and your career.

Key Takeaways

1. **Understand critical network components** such as switches, routers, firewalls, access points, and how they function within a network.

2. **Apply the OSI and TCP/IP models** to conceptualize and troubleshoot how data moves across network layers.

3. **Identify essential protocols and port numbers** like HTTP (80), HTTPS (443), DNS (53), DHCP (67/68), FTP (21), SSH (22), and SNMP (161/162).

4. **Recognize the format and purpose of IP addresses**, distinguishing between IPv4 and IPv6.

5. **Use CIDR notation and address classes** to determine IP ranges and subnet masks.

6. **Visualize how components and concepts interconnect**, forming a cohesive system that supports secure, scalable, and efficient communication.

Exam Tip #8

Use flashcards or repetition drills to reinforce port numbers and protocol names. Expect both direct recall and scenario-based exam questions.

CHAPTER 3

Network Implementations

Every network, whether used by a small business or a multinational enterprise, must be designed around the environment in which it operates. This design begins with determining what *type* of network will best serve the organization's goals. Different network types serve different needs—ranging from localized internal communication to global-scale connectivity—and each comes with its own set of protocols, technologies, and architectural requirements.

Understanding the distinctions between network types is critical for planning, maintaining, and scaling infrastructure. Equally important is grasping how data is physically and logically arranged through network topologies. Topology influences performance, scalability, fault tolerance, and even security posture. In this chapter, you'll learn how to differentiate common network types, identify where they're used, and understand their benefits and limitations. You'll also explore physical and logical topologies, which help determine how devices communicate within a given network layout.

Mastering these concepts is vital for both the CompTIA Network+ exam and for your practical growth as a networking professional.

© Kodi A. Cochran 2026

K. A. Cochran, *CompTIA Network+ (N10-009) Certification Companion,*
Certification Study Companion Series, https://doi.org/10.1007/979-8-8688-2341-1_3

Types of Networks

Network types are categorized based on geographic scope, ownership, and purpose. Understanding these classifications enables you to recommend or implement network solutions that are appropriate for specific environments and business needs.

Common Types of Networks:

- **Local Area Network (LAN):**
  - Covers a limited geographic area such as a home, office, or campus
  - High-speed connections with relatively low latency
  - Example: Office building network connecting computers and printers

- **Wide Area Network (WAN):**
  - It covers a large geographic area, often connecting multiple LANs.
  - Typically relies on leased telecommunication lines.
  - Example: A multinational corporation's network connecting offices across countries.

- **Metropolitan Area Network (MAN):**
  - Spans a city or large campus
  - Often owned by a consortium or service provider
  - Example: City-wide Wi-Fi services or university campuses

- **Campus Area Network (CAN):**
  - Interconnects multiple LANs within a limited geographic area, such as a university or business park
  - Typically, under a single organization's ownership
- **Personal Area Network (PAN):**
  - Very small network, typically within the range of a few meters.
  - Examples include Bluetooth connections between a smartphone and a headset.

Exam Tip #9

Be familiar with the differences between LANs, WANs, MANs, CANs, and PANs, especially regarding their size, ownership, and typical use cases. This foundational knowledge is often tested on the Network+ exam.

Wired Networking Standards

Wired networks provide high-speed, stable connections using physical cabling. Understanding cable types, speed capabilities, and distance limitations is essential when designing or upgrading a network.

Common Wired Media Types

- **Twisted Pair Cabling:**
  - Most common type for LAN connections

- Includes Unshielded Twisted Pair (UTP) and Shielded Twisted Pair (STP)

  - If you use STP, remember that the shielding only helps when it's properly grounded at the correct point; done wrong, you can actually introduce noise instead of reducing it.

- Examples: Cat5e, Cat6, Cat6a, Cat7

- **Coaxial Cable:**

  - Common coax types you'll run into include RG-6 (typical for cable broadband) and RG-59 (older installs and shorter runs).

    - Used traditionally for cable Internet and older networking.

    - Offers shielding and better resistance to electromagnetic interference.

- **Fiber Optic Cable:**

  - Transmits data using light rather than electrical signals.

  - Immune to electromagnetic interference.

  - Supports extremely high speeds and long distances.

Ethernet Standards Overview

Standard	Speed	Maximum distance	Media type
10BASE-T	10 Mbps	100 meters	Twisted pair
100BASE-TX	100 Mbps	100 meters	Twisted pair
1000BASE-T	1 Gbps	100 meters	Twisted pair
10GBASE-T	10 Gbps	55 meters (Cat6)	Twisted pair
10GBASE-SR	10 Gbps	300 meters (MMF)	Fiber optic
1000BASE-LX	1 Gbps	5 kilometers	Fiber optic

Exam Tip #10

Know the speeds, media types, and maximum distances associated with common Ethernet standards. Matching requirements to the appropriate cabling is a frequent exam scenario. A simple way to keep Ethernet standards straight is to build a one-page chart (or flashcards) comparing 100BASE-TX vs. 1000BASE-T vs. 10GBASE-SR—speed, media type, and max distance.

Wireless Networking Standards

Wireless networking offers flexibility and mobility that wired networks cannot match. Designing an efficient and secure wireless network requires understanding the different wireless standards and frequencies.

Common Wireless Standards

- **802.11a:**
  - Operates at 5 GHz

- Supports up to 54 Mbps

- Shorter range due to higher frequency

- **802.11b:**

  - Operates at 2.4 GHz

  - Supports up to 11 Mbps

  - Longer range but more prone to interference

- **802.11g:**

  - Operates at 2.4 GHz

  - Supports up to 54 Mbps

  - Backward compatible with 802.11b

- **802.11n:**

  - Operates at both 2.4 GHz and 5 GHz (dual-band)

  - Supports up to 600 Mbps with MIMO technology

- **802.11ac:**

  - Operates at 5 GHz

  - Supports up to 1 Gbps or higher with wider channels and MU-MIMO

- **802.11ax (Wi-Fi 6):**

  - Operates at both 2.4 GHz and 5 GHz

  - Supports speed up to 9.6 Gbps

  - Improved efficiency, capacity, and performance in dense environments

Exam Tip #11

Know which wireless standards operate at 2.4 GHz versus 5 GHz and be familiar with their speed capabilities and advantages.

Wireless Security Protocols

Wireless networks present unique security challenges. Unlike wired networks, which require physical access, wireless networks are more susceptible to unauthorized access and interception. To secure wireless communications, several protocols have been developed over the years, each improving upon the weaknesses of its predecessor. Security and compliance controls are primarily managed by the provider, though customers are still responsible for securing their applications and data.

Common Wireless Security Protocols

- **WEP (Wired Equivalent Privacy):**
    - The original security protocol for 802.11 WLANs
    - Uses RC4 encryption but suffers from major security flaws
    - Deprecated due to vulnerabilities and ease of cracking

- **WPA (Wi-Fi Protected Access):**
    - Introduced as an improvement over WEP
    - Uses TKIP (Temporal Key Integrity Protocol)
    - More secure than WEP but still vulnerable

- **WPA2:**

  - Mandatory use of AES (Advanced Encryption Standard).

  - Stronger security and improved performance over WPA.

  - It is still widely used in enterprise and consumer networks.

- **WPA3:**

  - Most current standard.

  - Uses SAE (Simultaneous Authentication of Equals) for more robust key exchange. In WPA3-Personal, SAE replaces the traditional PSK exchange and provides forward secrecy, so capturing traffic today doesn't automatically help an attacker decrypt it later if the password is compromised.

  - Improved protection against brute-force attacks and better security for public networks.

Exam Tip #12

Understand the evolution of wireless security protocols. Pay close attention to the differences between WEP, WPA, WPA2, and WPA3, especially regarding encryption methods and vulnerabilities.

Wireless Site Survey Basics

Designing an effective wireless network requires more than just placing access points (APs) throughout a building. Wireless signals are influenced by numerous environmental variables, and a well-executed site survey ensures the network delivers optimal performance, security, and reliability.

Key Survey Considerations

1. **Coverage:** Ensure the wireless signal reaches every intended area, accounting for square footage, floor layout, and wall materials.

2. **Capacity:** Consider the number of concurrent users and bandwidth demand in specific locations, such as conference rooms, lecture halls, or open-office environments.

3. **Channel Overlap:** Strategically assign non-overlapping channels (especially on 2.4 GHz bands) to minimize co-channel and adjacent-channel interference between nearby APs. On the 2.4 GHz band, channels 1, 6, and 11 are the only non-overlapping set in most environments; the 5 GHz band offers more non-overlapping options, which helps reduce interference in dense deployments.

4. **Signal Strength (RSSI):** Use site survey tools and heat maps to measure Received Signal Strength Indicator (RSSI) across the coverage area, ensuring consistent and strong signal quality.

5. **Obstructions and Interference:** Identify physical barriers (e.g., concrete walls, glass, metal structures) and electronic interference sources (e.g., microwaves, cordless phones) that can degrade wireless performance.

Signal quality is also influenced by signal-to-noise ratio (SNR). A strong RSSI does not help much if the noise floor is high, so consider both metrics when diagnosing wireless performance. Keep in mind RSSI is not standardized—vendors report it differently—so interpret readings in the context of your specific equipment.

Types of Wireless Site Surveys

1. **Passive Survey:**

   - Measures existing wireless signals without connecting to a specific AP.

   - Passive surveys also help detect rogue access points and external interference by enumerating nearby SSIDs, channels, and signal levels.

   - Ideal for mapping signal strength and identifying interference.

   - Common tools: Ekahau, NetSpot, AirMagnet.

2. **Active Survey:**

   - Connects to an AP to gather performance metrics (e.g., throughput, packet loss, latency)

   - Useful for validating end user experience and diagnosing performance issues

3. **Predictive Survey:**

   - Uses building blueprints and RF modeling software to simulate signal propagation before deployment

   - Cost-effective for new deployments or renovations, especially in large environments

Exam Tip #13

Be familiar with the goals and tools used in wireless site surveys. Know when to use each survey type and how to address common issues like interference, dead zones, and signal degradation.

Network Topologies

Network topologies describe how devices are connected and how data travels across a network. These layouts influence performance, fault tolerance, scalability, and ease of troubleshooting. Understanding both physical and logical topologies is essential when designing or analyzing network structures.

Physical vs. Logical Topologies

1. **Physical topology** describes the actual physical connections (e.g., cables, switches). These are all items that you can physically see and touch.

2. **Logical topology** describes how data flows regardless of physical layout.

In practice, logical topology is governed by Layer 2 and Layer 3 behavior—Ethernet switching (MAC forwarding) and IP routing determine the actual data path through the network.

Common Topologies

1. **Bus Topology:**

   - All devices connect to a single backbone cable.

- Inexpensive but prone to collisions and difficult to troubleshoot. Bus topology is largely obsolete today and mainly appears in legacy environments or exam questions.

2. **Star Topology:**

- Devices connect to a central switch or hub.

- Easy to manage and scalable.

- Most common topology in modern LANs.

3. **Ring Topology:**

- Devices connected in a circular fashion.

- Each device has exactly two neighbors.

- One device failure can disrupt the whole network unless dual rings are used.

4. **Mesh Topology:**

- Devices are interconnected for redundancy.

- Provides high fault tolerance.

- Used in WANs and mission-critical environments.

5. **Hybrid Topology:**

- Combines two or more topologies (e.g., star-bus)

- Offers flexibility and scalability

Exam Tip #14

Be able to identify topologies based on visual diagrams and understand their pros and cons, especially in terms of fault tolerance, cost, and scalability.

Common Networking Devices

Understanding core networking devices is essential for building, securing, and managing modern networks. Each device serves a distinct purpose, operates at a specific OSI layer, and contributes to the overall communication and functionality of the network.

Key Networking Devices

1. **Hub:**

    - Operates at OSI Layer 1 (Physical Layer).

    - Broadcasts all incoming traffic to every port regardless of destination.

    - Offers no traffic filtering or intelligence. Because it does not learn MAC addresses or maintain a forwarding table, a hub cannot make intelligent forwarding decisions.

    - Obsolete in modern networks due to inefficiency and collision risk. Because hubs cannot make MAC-based forwarding decisions, they flood traffic and increase the chance of collisions on shared segments.

2. **Switch:**

   - Operates at OSI Layer 2 (Data Link Layer)

   - Forwards traffic intelligently using MAC address tables

   - Reduces collisions and improves performance

   - Common in almost all LAN environments

3. **Router:**

   - Operates at OSI Layer 3 (Network Layer)

   - Directs packets between different networks using IP addresses

   - Supports NAT, DHCP, and basic firewall functions

   - Core component of both home and enterprise network infrastructures

4. **Access Point (AP):**

   - Extends a wired network by providing wireless access

   - Functions as a bridge between wireless clients and the wired LAN

   - May support features such as SSID broadcasting, security protocols, and multiple frequency bands

5. **Modem:**

   - Short for "modulator-demodulator."

- Handles modulation and demodulation to carry data over provider media such as coax (DOCSIS), DSL, or fiber handoffs (ONUs/ONTs). In modern broadband, this is largely digital signaling, but the term "modem" persists from legacy terminology. Unlike legacy dial-up, modern DOCSIS and fiber ONTs are not doing the classic analog conversion people associate with early modems, but the name stuck.

- It is used to connect local networks to ISPs.

6. **Firewall:**

  - Inspects and filters traffic based on predefined security rules

  - Can be implemented in hardware, software, or as a hybrid

  - Protects networks from unauthorized access and threats

Exam Tip #15

Be able to match each device to its function and corresponding OSI layer. This foundational knowledge is frequently tested and supports effective troubleshooting.

Structured Cabling and Distribution

A well-designed cabling infrastructure provides the foundation for scalable, reliable, and easily maintained networks. Structured cabling systems follow established standards to ensure consistency, support troubleshooting, and promote interoperability among equipment.

Key Concepts

1. **TIA/EIA-568 Standard:**

    - Defines standards for wiring, pinouts, and cable labeling

    - Includes specifications for horizontal and backbone cabling

2. **568A and 568B Pinouts:**

    - Define color coding for Ethernet cable wiring

    - Must match on both ends for straight-through cables

3. **MDF (Main Distribution Frame):**

    - Central point of connection for external service provider circuits

    - Connects to IDFs

4. **IDF (Intermediate Distribution Frame):**

    - Located on individual floors or buildings

    - Connects endpoints to the MDF via backbone cabling

Exam Tip #16

Be able to recognize structured cabling standards and their practical applications in enterprise networks.

Cloud Deployment Models

Cloud deployment models define how cloud resources are provisioned, accessed, and managed depending on an organization's specific requirements for control, security, compliance, and scalability. Each model offers distinct trade-offs in terms of cost, flexibility, and responsibility, and understanding these models is essential for designing and securing cloud infrastructure. Typically requires significant capital expenditure and skilled staff for deployment and maintenance.

Public Cloud

1. The infrastructure is owned and operated by third-party providers who deliver services over the Internet.

2. Offers on-demand scalability, reduced upfront costs, and simplified management. Public cloud is typically an operational expense (OpEx) model, where you pay for what you use instead of purchasing the hardware up front.

3. Resources such as storage, computer power, and applications are shared across multiple customers (multi-tenancy).

4. Security and compliance controls are primarily managed by the provider, though customers are still responsible for securing their applications and data. This is commonly described as the cloud shared responsibility model: the provider secures the underlying infrastructure, while you secure your identities, configurations, data, and workloads.

5. Best suited for dynamic workloads, start-ups, or businesses with minimal regulatory concerns.

6. **Examples:** Amazon Web Services (AWS), Microsoft Azure, Google Cloud Platform (GCP).

Private Cloud

1. Infrastructure is dedicated to a single organization and may be hosted on-premises or off-site by a third-party provider.

2. Offers maximum control over hardware, networking, data security, and compliance.

3. Enables full customization to meet specific business or regulatory requirements.

4. Typically requires significant capital expenditure and skilled staff for deployment and maintenance. In other words, private cloud investments are usually capital expense-(CapEx)heavy, with ongoing operational costs for staff and maintenance.

5. Best suited for government agencies, financial institutions, and companies handling sensitive data.

Hybrid Cloud

1. Integrates public and private cloud environments to allow seamless data and application movement between them.

2. Enables organizations to leverage public cloud for burst workloads or non-sensitive operations while retaining critical data in private infrastructure.

3. Supports disaster recovery, high availability, and load balancing strategies.

4. Requires careful orchestration and integration tools to ensure interoperability. In practice, organizations often use toolsets from VMware, AWS, and Azure (e.g., VMware vSphere/NSX, AWS Outposts, or Azure Arc) to manage hybrid connectivity and consistent policy enforcement.

5. Offers balance between flexibility and control—ideal for enterprises with both legacy and cloud-native applications.

Community Cloud

1. Infrastructure is shared between several organizations with similar operational or regulatory needs (e.g., data sovereignty, compliance frameworks).

2. Often used by entities in the same sector, such as healthcare, government, or education.

3. Managed collectively by the participating organizations or by a designated third party.

4. Offers cost efficiency and shared responsibility while meeting common compliance standards.

5. Less common than other models but growing in relevance as industry-specific compliance demands increase.

Exam Tip #17

Be familiar with the characteristics and use cases of each cloud deployment model. Questions may ask which model best suits a particular business scenario or compliance requirement. Match the appropriate cloud model to a scenario based on security needs, cost, and scalability.

Virtualization and Cloud Networking

Modern network environments rely heavily on virtualization and cloud technologies to maximize resource efficiency, support scalability, and enable dynamic service delivery. These technologies abstract physical hardware to allow flexible deployments, cost savings, and centralized management across distributed environments.

Virtualization Concepts

1. **Hypervisors:** Software platforms that create and manage virtual machines (VMs).

   - *Type 1 hypervisors* (bare metal) run directly on hardware and are typically used in enterprise environments (e.g., VMware ESXi, Microsoft Hyper-V Server).

   - *Type 2 hypervisors* run on top of a host operating system and are used in workstations or test environments (e.g., Oracle VirtualBox, VMware Workstation).

2. **Virtual Machines (VMs):** Emulated systems that behave like independent physical computers. Each VM operates its own guest OS, runs applications, and uses virtualized hardware resources (CPU, memory, storage, NICs).

3. **Virtual Switches:** Software-based switches embedded within hypervisors that allow inter-VM communication and connection to physical networks. They can support VLANs, traffic filtering, and segmentation policies. A virtual switch operates primarily at OSI Layer 2 (MAC switching) and may support features such as trunking, port mirroring, and—depending on the platform—NIC teaming.

4. **Snapshots and Cloning:** Virtualization platforms allow administrators to capture point-in-time snapshots for short-term rollback and to create duplicate systems (clones) for migration, testing, and lab replication. Snapshots are not a backup and should not replace a proper backup strategy.

Cloud Computing Models

1. **Infrastructure as a Service (IaaS):** Provides basic infrastructure, computer, storage, and networking—on-demand. Customers manage their own OS and applications, while the provider manages the underlying hardware.

   - ***Example:*** Amazon EC2, Microsoft Azure Virtual Machines

2. **Platform as a Service (PaaS):** Offers development and deployment platforms with managed infrastructure. Developers focus on building applications without managing servers or operating systems.

- ***Example:*** Google App Engine, Microsoft Azure App Services

3. **Software as a Service (SaaS):** Delivers fully developed applications accessible via web browsers. Users interact with the software while the provider manages everything, including infrastructure, platform, and updates.

   - ***Example:*** Microsoft 365, Salesforce, Dropbox

Benefits of Virtualization and Cloud Networking

1. Significant cost savings through reduced hardware expenditure

2. Efficient use of computing resources via dynamic allocation and pooling

3. Rapid provisioning and scaling of applications and services

4. Simplified disaster recovery and business continuity planning

5. Easier testing and deployment through environment replication

Exam Tip #18

Understand the roles of hypervisors and virtual machines in modern networks. Be able to differentiate between IaaS, PaaS, and SaaS by who manages what layers of the stack and which model fits a given business scenario.

Chapter Summary

In Chapter 3, you examined the critical building blocks that define how modern networks are designed, deployed, and managed. You started by differentiating between core network types—such as LANs, WANs, MANs, CANs, and PANs—based on size, geographic scope, administrative control, and usage scenarios. Understanding these distinctions is essential when selecting the appropriate architecture for business and organizational needs.

You then explored the physical and logical topologies that determine how devices connect and communicate. From traditional bus and ring layouts to the more scalable and fault-tolerant mesh and star designs, each topology presents unique advantages and limitations. Recognizing the impact of these configurations on performance and reliability is crucial for both troubleshooting and planning.

Next, you reviewed the foundational components of wired and wireless networks. This included an in-depth look at twisted pair, coaxial, and fiber optic cables, along with key Ethernet standards such as 100BASE-T and 10GBASE-SR. You also studied 802.11 wireless standards—like 802.11n, 802.11ac, and Wi-Fi 6 (802.11ax)—and how frequency, bandwidth, and backward compatibility influence wireless deployment. Security was addressed through a breakdown of wireless encryption protocols, including the progression from WEP to WPA3. You learned how these protocols differ in encryption strength, authentication methods, and vulnerability mitigation, helping ensure secure wireless communication.

The chapter also emphasized virtualization and cloud technologies. You studied hypervisors (Type 1 and Type 2), virtual machines, virtual switches, and snapshots—all of which enable scalable, flexible environments. You compared cloud service models—Infrastructure as a Service (IaaS), Platform as a Service (PaaS), and Software as a Service (SaaS) as well as cloud deployment types such as public, private, hybrid, and community cloud. Wireless site survey methodologies were introduced as a critical step in designing efficient wireless environments. You learned the difference between passive, active, and predictive surveys and how tools like heat maps and spectrum analyzers contribute to identifying signal strength, channel overlap, and physical interference.

This chapter laid the groundwork for understanding how modern networks function, scale, and secure communications across physical and cloud-based infrastructures. In the real world, this is the knowledge you rely on as a network technician, junior system administrator, or cloud support associate—choosing the right design, understanding the trade-offs, and troubleshooting when the environment doesn't behave like the diagram.

Key Takeaways

1. Differentiate between LANs, WANs, MANs, CANs, and PANs based on scale, control, and typical use cases.

2. Understand physical and logical topologies and how they affect network performance, scalability, and fault tolerance.

3. Identify media types, including twisted pair, coaxial, and fiber optics, and relate them to relevant Ethernet standards.

4. Compare wireless standards (802.11a/b/g/n/a/ax) by frequency, bandwidth, and backward compatibility.

5. Evaluate wireless security protocols from WEP to WPA3, focusing on encryption methods and known vulnerabilities.

6. Explain the roles of hypervisors, virtual machines, and virtual switches in network virtualization.

7. Distinguish between IaaS, PaaS, and SaaS based on control, responsibility, and use case.

8. Understand cloud deployment models (public, private, hybrid, community) and their advantages for scalability, cost, and security.

9. Apply wireless site survey strategies to identify coverage gaps, channel overlap, and environmental interference.

Exam Tip #19

Expect exam scenarios that ask you to match network types or topologies to real-world designs, select appropriate media and standards, choose between virtualization/cloud models, and identify which wireless protocol or site survey method fits a given deployment.

CHAPTER 4

Network Operations

A well-functioning network is not just the result of quality hardware or solid configuration, it depends on consistent, proactive operations management. Network operations encompass the daily tasks, procedures, and policies that ensure ongoing stability, performance, and security of network environments. This includes monitoring and documentation, change management, disaster recovery planning, and policy enforcement.

At the heart of effective network operations is documentation. Without clear and accurate records of device configurations, logical and physical layouts, IP address allocations, and change histories, even simple troubleshooting tasks can become time-consuming and error-prone. Comprehensive documentation ensures that teams can quickly board new staff, pass audits, meet regulatory requirements, and make informed decisions about scaling or upgrading the infrastructure.

But network operations go far beyond documentation. This chapter also explores how to implement robust monitoring systems, apply configuration baselines, automate routine tasks, and prepare for emergencies. Whether responding to a sudden network outage, applying a security patch, or tracking bandwidth usage, IT professionals rely on standardized operational practices to maintain network health.

By mastering the principles of network operations, you will not only reduce downtime and improve user satisfaction but also gain the ability to anticipate and prevent problems before they impact business continuity.

© Kodi A. Cochran 2026
K. A. Cochran, *CompTIA Network+ (N10-009) Certification Companion,*
Certification Study Companion Series, https://doi.org/10.1007/979-8-8688-2341-1_4

In this chapter, you will

- Learn the importance of accurate and up-to-date network documentation

- Explore the fundamentals of network monitoring and performance analysis

- Understand configuration management and change control best practices

- Review the components of disaster recovery and business continuity planning

- Examine how automation and standard operating procedures enhance operational efficiency

These operational skills are critical to the real-world role of a network professional and represent a major component of the CompTIA Network+ certification exam.

Types of Network Documentation

Network documentation is a core element of operations that supports planning, troubleshooting, auditing, and overall infrastructure management. Different types of documentation serve different operational needs, and a complete documentation system should incorporate all of the following:

- **Physical Network Diagrams**

  - Illustrate the physical layout of the network, including device locations, cabling paths, patch panels, racks, and wiring closets.

  - Help technicians trace connections, plan hardware installations, and quickly locate network components during outages or maintenance.

- **Logical Network Diagrams**

  - Represent the logical structure of the network, such as IP address schemes, subnets, VLAN assignments, routing relationships, and firewall zones.

  - Useful for understanding how data flows between devices, planning network segmentation, and auditing network design against security policies.

- **Configuration Documentation**

  - Includes saved configuration files for switches, routers, firewalls, wireless controllers, and other devices

  - Also, records firmware versions, authentication methods, access credentials (secured), and routing or NAT policies

  - Enables rollback to known good states, simplifies compliance audits, and speeds up recovery after a failure

- **IP Address Management (IPAM)**

  - Tracks allocation and usage of IP addresses across the organization

  - Includes subnet maps, DHCP scopes, static address assignments, and address reservations

  - Prevents conflicts, ensures availability, and aids in future network expansion or redesign

- **Inventory Lists**

  - Catalog hardware (e.g., switches, servers, access points) and software (e.g., operating systems, licenses).

  - Include serial numbers, device models, physical locations, purchase dates, warranty periods, and software keys.

  - Helps streamline procurement, maintenance schedules, and end-of-life planning.

Properly maintained network documentation not only improves operational visibility but also forms the backbone of disaster recovery, training, and incident response protocols.

Best Practices for Documentation

To ensure your documentation remains useful, accurate, and secure, consider implementing the following best practices:

- **Use standardized templates and diagramming conventions.**

  - Ensure consistency across all documents and diagrams.

  - Follow industry-recognized symbols and layouts for readability and universal understanding.

- **Store documentation securely with controlled access.**

  - This also includes how you handle credentials. Never store passwords, shared secrets, or SNMP

community strings in plain text inside diagrams
or runbooks. Reference them through a password
manager or secrets vault instead.

- Use centralized repositories with version
  control and access logs.

- Restrict access to sensitive configuration
  and security documentation to authorized
  personnel only.

- **Update documentation after every change or audit.**

  - Treat documentation as a living resource. Outdated
    diagrams or configurations can mislead technicians
    and create risk.

  - Implement changing tracking to associate updates
    with specific events or maintenance windows.

- **Integrate documentation with monitoring and
  ticketing systems.**

  - Link real-time device data and incident history with
    static documentation to create a more dynamic and
    responsive operational environment.

  - Allow technicians to access related documents
    directly from trouble tickets or alerts.

Following these practices ensures that documentation serves its
purpose as a reliable, secure, and up-to-date resource across all phases of
network operations.

Exam Tip #20

Be familiar with the distinctions between physical and logical network diagrams. Documentation is a foundational part of network operations and often referenced in exam questions involving troubleshooting or implementation planning.

Change Management

Change management is a structured and disciplined process for introducing modifications to a network in a controlled and risk-mitigated way. Rather than ad hoc configuration tweaks or emergency fixes, formal change management ensures that each modification—no matter how small—is properly documented, reviewed, tested, communicated, and validated. This reduces unplanned downtime, prevents security misconfigurations, and ensures accountability across teams.

Network environments are dynamic—software updates, hardware replacements, policy changes, and new services are all part of normal operations. However, each of these introduces potential for disruption, if not handled carefully. An effective change management framework is critical to maintaining operational stability while allowing innovation and improvement.

Stages of a Robust Change Management Life Cycle

1. **Change Request Submission**

   - Initiators must complete a formal Change Request (CR) form detailing the nature, purpose, affected systems, timeline, and potential risks of the proposed change.

- Each request should include

  - Business justification

  - Risk level (low, medium, high)

  - Scope of impact

  - Rollback and contingency procedures

2. **Technical and Business Review**

   - A Change Advisory Board (CAB)—comprising network engineers, system admins, project managers, and possibly security and compliance officers—evaluates the request.

   - Review focuses on technical feasibility, alignment with organizational strategy, cost, downtime risks, and compliance with standards.

3. **Testing and Validation**

   - Prior to deployment, changes should be replicated in a test or staging environment that closely mirrors production.

   - This stage evaluates

     - Interoperability with existing systems

     - Performance benchmarks

     - Effects on dependencies and integrations

     - Potential security implications

4. **Approval and Scheduling**

- After successful review and testing, approved changes are scheduled for implementation.

- Timing is chosen to minimize business impact (typically during off-hours or designated maintenance windows).

- All implementation tasks are documented in a deployment plan, including estimated duration, personnel assignments, and success/failure criteria.

5. **Communication and Stakeholder Notification**

- Relevant stakeholders, including IT support teams, department heads, help desk staff, and end users, are informed of

    - The nature and purpose of the change

    - Timing and expected duration

    - Potential service disruptions

    - Contact information for escalation

6. **Implementation and Real-Time Tracking**

- The change is implemented according to the approved deployment plan.

- Administrators document progress, results, unexpected behavior, and deviations in real time to support transparency and future analysis.

7. **Post-Implementation Review (PIR)**

- Once the change is applied, network functionality is validated through

    - Log review

    - Monitoring tools

    - End user feedback

- Any issues are triaged immediately and, if necessary, the change is rolled back using the predefined contingency plan.

8. **Documentation and Lessons Learned**

- The change, its outcomes, and any issues encountered are formally documented.

- Lessons learned should be reviewed during CAB meetings or internal team reviews to improve future management processes.

Change management should not be viewed as red tape—it is a critical safeguard for network integrity. By balancing control with agility, it allows organizations to evolve their infrastructure in a way that minimizes risk and supports long-term operational excellence.

Types of Network Changes

Not all changes are created equally, different types of modifications require different levels of oversight, documentation, and urgency. Categorizing changes appropriately ensures that the right processes are followed, risk is managed appropriately, and resources are allocated efficiently.

1. **Standard Changes**

    - Pre-approved, low-risk changes that follow a repeatable process

    - Examples include routine firmware updates, updating inventory records, adding VLANs to a switch, or modifying access control lists based on known templates

    - Typically require minimal documentation and do not need CAB approval if they meet pre-defined criteria

2. **Emergency Changes**

    - High-priority modifications made in response to unexpected issues that threaten network stability, security, or business operations

    - Examples include patching a zero-day vulnerability, restoring failed equipment, or rerouting traffic during an outage

    - May bypass certain stages of the approval process but still require post-implementation documentation and review

3. **Major Changes**

    - High-impact or high-complexity changes involving multiple systems, teams, or critical services

    - Require thorough planning, extended testing, full CAB approval, and scheduled maintenance windows

- Examples include core switch replacements, network segmentation projects, or changes to routing architecture

Best Practices for Change Management

To ensure changes are implemented effectively and responsibly, organizations should adhere to proven best practices:

1. **Engage Stakeholders Throughout the Life Cycle**

   - Involve relevant technical teams, business units, and users from the planning phase through validation.

   - This ensures alignment with operational goals and prevents overlooked items that may otherwise not be considered.

2. **Automate Workflows When Possible.**

   - Use change management software or IT service management (ITSM) platforms to streamline approvals, reminders, and status tracking.

   - Automation helps reduce human error and improves consistency.

3. **Maintain an Immutable Change Log.**

   - Keep detailed, time-stamped records of every change, including who initiated it, what was done, when, and the outcome.

   - A historical log supports auditing, compliance, incident response, and organizational memory.

4. **Use Change Templates for Recurring Tasks.**

   - Develop standardized procedures for common changes to reduce planning time and improve predictability.

5. **Schedule and Communicate in Advance.**

   - Avoid surprise outages by publishing change calendars and communicating expected impacts well before implementation.

Exam Tip #21

Know the roles, steps, and types of change processes. The difference between emergency, standard, and major changes is often tested, especially in scenarios involving troubleshooting or deployment coordination.

Disaster Recovery Procedures

Disaster recovery (DR) is a critical subset of business continuity planning focused on restoring IT infrastructure and services after a significant disruption. Whether caused by natural disasters, cyberattacks, system failures, or human error, the goal of disaster recovery is to return operations to a functional state quickly and efficiently—minimizing data loss, downtime, and revenue impact.

An effective disaster recovery plan (DRP) is more than just backup; it is a well-documented, thoroughly tested strategy that aligns technical recovery capabilities with organizational priorities.

Key Components of a Disaster Recovery Plan

1. **Business Impact Analysis (BIA)**

   - Identifies mission-critical systems, services, and processes

   - Analyzes the potential consequences of prolonged outages (financial loss, regulatory penalties, customer dissatisfaction).

   - Prioritizes systems for recovery based on their importance to operations

2. **Risk Assessment**

   - Evaluates both internal and external threats to IT services

   - Includes natural disasters (floods, fires), hardware failures, malware attacks, insider threats, and third-party failures

   - Determines likelihood and impact to guide investment in preventive and recovery measures

3. **Recovery Time Objective (RTO)**

   - Defines the maximum acceptable amount of time that a system or application can be down after a disaster before causing significant harm

   - Helps determine urgency and resource allocation for system recovery efforts

4. **Recovery Point Objective (RPO)**

   - Specifies the maximum amount of data (measured in time) that can be lost without significant impact.

   - For example, an RPO of 4 hours means backups must occur at least every four hours to meet data retention requirements.

5. **Backup Strategy:** Know the trade-offs: full backups take the longest to run but restore the fastest; incremental backups are quick to run but restore the slowest because you must apply the last full plus every incremental in the chain; differential backups usually restore faster than incremental (last full + latest differential), but grow larger over time and therefore take longer to run as the days pass.

   - Outlines the type, frequency, and location of backups:

     1. **Full backup**: A complete copy of all data

     2. **Incremental backup**: Captures changes since the last backup

     3. **Differential backup**: Captures all changes since the last full backup

   - May use a combination of on-site storage, off-site facilities, and cloud services for redundancy and geographic diversity

6. **Disaster Recovery Sites**

   - **Hot Site:** Fully operational replica of the primary site with real-time data synchronization. Provides near-instant failover but is costly to maintain.

- **Warm Site:** Partially equipped facility with pre-installed hardware and regularly updated backups. Recovery time is longer but more cost-effective than a hot site.

- **Cold Site:** An empty facility with power and connectivity but no equipment or data. Least expensive option, but longest recovery time.

7. **Testing and Training**

- Regular DR testing (tabletop exercises, simulations, and full-scale drills) validates the effectiveness of the plan and uncovers gaps.

- Staff should be trained in their roles within the DR plan to ensure rapid and coordinated response during an actual event.

Best Practices for Disaster Recovery

1. **Integrate DR with Broader Business Continuity Plans.**

- Disaster recovery should not exist in isolation— it should support overall organizational resilience goals.

- Coordinate with HR, facilities, and executive leadership to align IT recovery with business continuity strategies.

2. **Automate Where Possible**

- Use technologies such as continuous data protection (CDP), automated failover clusters, and backup scheduling tools to reduce human error and accelerate recovery.

3. **Document and Rehearse the Plan**

- Ensure DR documentation is accessible during emergencies and reflects current infrastructure.

- Include detailed contact lists, procedures, system diagrams, and access credentials (stored securely).

4. **Review and Update Regularly**

- Conduct quarterly or biannual reviews to account for infrastructure changes, personnel updates, and emerging threats.

Exam Tip #22

Be able to differentiate between RTO and RPO, and understand the differences between hot, warm, and cold disaster recovery sites. Expect scenario-based questions about disaster preparedness and continuity planning.

Monitoring Tools and Performance Metrics

Network monitoring is a proactive discipline that enables IT teams to maintain performance, prevent outages, and ensure service-level objectives are met. Rather than waiting for users to report issues, robust monitoring systems provide real-time visibility into the health of network infrastructure, helping teams detect anomalies, track usage trends, and respond to problems before they escalate.

A successful monitoring strategy combines the right tools with clearly defined metrics and thresholds. Together, these allow organizations to optimize network operations and support business continuity. Avoid excessive or irrelevant alerts by setting realistic, tiered thresholds for key metrics. Protect SNMP access with SNMPv3, disable unnecessary protocols, and secure access to monitoring servers.

Core Monitoring Tools and Technologies

1. **SNMP (Simple Network Management Protocol)**

   - A widely adopted protocol that allows network administrators to poll and configure devices remotely.

   - SNMP agents embedded in routers, switches, servers, and printers report performance data (e.g., CPU usage, interface errors, link status).

   - Supports automated alerts (*traps*) when thresholds are breached, enabling immediate response.

2. **Syslog**

   - A standardized logging protocol used to send system and event messages from network devices to a centralized log collector or SIEM (Security Information and Event Management) system.

   - Events are classified by severity (e.g., emergency, critical, warning, info) to support filtering and prioritization.

   - Enables retrospective analysis, auditing, and incident response.

3. **NetFlow and sFlow**

- Flow-based telemetry systems that monitor conversations between endpoints (e.g., source/destination IPs, ports, protocols).

- Useful for identifying high-bandwidth consumers, unusual traffic spikes, and DDoS attacks.

- NetFlow is primarily Cisco-based, while sFlow is vendor-neutral.

4. **Packet Analyzers (e.g., Wireshark)**

- Provide in-depth packet-level inspection by capturing and decoding traffic.

- Critical for troubleshooting application-layer issues, validating protocol handshakes, or investigating suspicious activity.

- Can analyze traffic in real time or post-capture, with support for filters and color-coded views.

5. **Integrated Network Monitoring Platforms**

- Tools like **SolarWinds**, **PRTG**, **Zabbix**, and **Nagios** combine multiple protocols (SNMP, Syslog, NetFlow) into unified dashboards.

- Offer alerting, historical data analysis, SLA compliance reports, and graphical performance visualizations.

- Some platforms include auto-discovery, topology mapping, and REST API integration with ticketing systems like ServiceNow.

Quick Tool-Selection Guide

1. **Device status and interface statistics:** SNMP polling via an NMS platform (often paired with dashboards and threshold-based alerting)

2. **Security incident review and auditing:** Centralized logs (Syslog) and a SIEM for search, correlation, and retention

3. **Flow analysis:** NetFlow/sFlow collectors to understand who is talking to whom, where bandwidth is going, and what "normal" looks like

4. **Deep packet inspection:** Packet capture and protocol decoding (packet analyzers), often using SPAN/port mirroring or taps to capture traffic at the right point

Critical Network Performance Metrics

1. **Latency**

   - The time taken for a data packet to travel from source to destination and back (round-trip time).

   - Excessive latency affects interactive applications like VoIP and online gaming.

2. **Jitter**

   - The variation in latency over time; high jitter leads to choppy audio or video in real-time applications.

   - Often caused by queuing delays or inconsistent packet paths.

3. **Packet Loss**

- Indicates dropped packets due to congestion, faulty hardware, or signal degradation

- Degrades the performance of TCP sessions and may result in retransmissions and timeouts

4. **Bandwidth Utilization**

- The percentage of the total available bandwidth that is being used at a given time.

- Sustained high utilization may indicate the need for link upgrades or QoS enforcement.

5. **Throughput**

- Measures the actual data rate achieved over the network, factoring in retransmissions and protocol overhead

- Reflects the efficiency of end-to-end communication under real-world conditions

Best Practices for Monitoring

1. **Define Performance Baselines**

- Establish normal behavior patterns for traffic volumes, latency, and interface loads.

- Use baselines to recognize anomalies such as memory leaks, failing hardware, or configuration errors.

2. **Configure Intelligent Alerts**

   - Avoid excessive or irrelevant alerts by setting realistic, tiered thresholds for key metrics. This reduces alert fatigue and helps teams stay responsive to high-impact events.

   - Differentiate between warning, critical, and informational alerts to prioritize incident response.

3. **Analyze Long-Term Trends**

   - Use historical monitoring data for capacity planning, hardware refresh cycles, and evaluating the impact of network changes.

4. **Harden Monitoring Infrastructure**

   - Protect SNMP access with SNMPv3, disable insecure versions (v1/v2c), and secure access to monitoring servers.

   - Isolate management traffic from production using VLANs or out-of-band networks.

5. **Incorporate Visualization and Reporting**

   - Use heat maps, graphs, and dashboard views to quickly interpret large volumes of data.

   - Automated reporting assists with compliance reviews, executive summaries, and vendor accountability.

Exam Tip #23

Expect scenario-based questions that ask which tool to use in a given situation—such as diagnosing latency, reviewing logs, capturing packets, or analyzing bandwidth. Understand how each monitoring method fits into a broader operational and security context.

Network Availability and Fault Tolerance Techniques

High availability (HA) and fault tolerance are core objectives of enterprise networking. While high availability emphasizes continuous service uptime, fault tolerance focuses on the ability to withstand and recover from hardware or software failures. Together, these principles minimize downtime, ensure data integrity, and protect the organization from service interruptions that could result in financial or reputational harm. Designing for availability requires proactive planning and the implementation of technologies that anticipate failures rather than merely respond to them.

Common Techniques and Technologies

Redundancy

1. Deploys multiple instances of critical hardware or systems—such as power supplies, NICs, ISPs, or switches—to eliminate single points of failure.

2. May include redundant hardware paths (dual power, dual WAN), redundant data paths (STP or VRRP), and redundant topologies (e.g., ring or mesh).

3. Redundancy can be implemented at the component level or across entire systems.

Load Balancing

1. Distributes network or application traffic across multiple servers or paths to balance demand and reduce strain on any one resource

2. It can be hardware-based (dedicated appliances) or software-defined (DNS-based or reverse proxy)

3. Improves both fault tolerance and performance, often used with web servers, VPN concentrators, and mail servers

Failover Systems

1. Automatically redirect services or workloads to backup systems in the event of failure.

2. Examples include high-availability pairs for firewalls, router HSRP (Hot Standby Router Protocol), or standby database nodes.

3. Failover systems may rely on heartbeats or monitoring daemons to detect failure conditions.

Clustering

1. Groups multiple servers or nodes to act as a single logical system.

2. Supports both load balancing and high availability; if one node fails, others in the cluster continue processing.

3. Used in file servers, virtualization hosts, and database management systems.

Link Aggregation (LAG)

1. Combines multiple network connections into a single logical link using protocols such as LACP (Link Aggregation Control Protocol).

2. Provides redundancy and increases bandwidth between switches, servers, or storage devices.

3. If one link in the group fails, traffic continues to flow through the remaining links.

Uninterruptible Power Supply (UPS)

1. Provides temporary power to critical systems during outages, allowing for graceful shutdown or failover

2. Can be paired with generators for longer outages

3. Also protects against voltage fluctuations and brownouts

Service Level Agreements (SLAs)

1. Formal contracts between businesses and service providers (e.g., ISPs, cloud vendors) defining expected performance metrics

2. May specify

   - A useful rule of thumb: "Five nines" (99.999%) works out to roughly five minutes of allowable downtime per year.

     1. Maximum time to repair (MTTR)

     2. Response times and escalation paths

3. Critical for managing expectations and ensuring accountability in third-party services.

Best Practices for High Availability

Regularly Monitor Redundant Components

- Redundancy only works if backup systems are operational. Use monitoring tools to verify link, power, and hardware status.

Perform Scheduled Failover Testing

- Conduct planned switchover events to confirm that failover systems are activated as expected.

- Test both automatic and manual recovery scenarios.

Availability with Application Criticality

- Not all services require 24/7 uptime. Tailor fault-tolerance strategies based on the business impact of each system.

- Apply greater resilience to systems like customer portals, VoIP infrastructure, and payment gateways.

Document HA and DR Configurations

- Maintain detailed records of high availability designs, including IP schemes, failover priorities, failback procedures, and dependencies.

- Store documentation securely and make it accessible to relevant staff during emergencies.

Combine Physical and Logical Redundancy

- Use both infrastructure-level redundancy (e.g., dual power circuits, diverse cable paths) and logical configurations (e.g., VRRP, BGP failover) for comprehensive protection.

Exam Tip #24

Understand how each technology contributes to uptime. The exam
may present a failure scenario and ask which solution—load balancer,
redundant link, UPS, or cluster—best maintains availability. Be prepared to
match fault-tolerance techniques with their appropriate use cases.

Configuration Management Tools

Configuration management refers to the standardized and automated
control of system settings, device configurations, and infrastructure
policies across a network. As environments scale in complexity, manual
configuration becomes error-prone and inefficient. Configuration
management tools help automate, track, and enforce consistent
setups across routers, switches, firewalls, and servers—reducing
misconfigurations and ensuring compliance with operational and security
policies.

These tools are essential for environments practicing Infrastructure
as Code (IaC), DevOps, or agile networking, where rapid deployment and
consistency are crucial.

Protect configuration tools and store credentials by restricting who can
view or modify specific device settings.

Popular Configuration Management Tools

Ansible

- Agentless automation platform developed by Red Hat

- Uses simple, human-readable YAML syntax called
  "playbooks"

- Pushes configuration to devices over SSH (or WinRM for Windows)

- Ideal for network automation and low-complexity, repeatable tasks

Puppet

- Uses a declarative language to define desired states

- Employs an agent/master model where managed nodes check in with a central server

- Good for environments that require continuous state enforcement and reporting

- Popular in large-scale infrastructure with complex interdependencies

Chef

- Uses a Ruby-based Domain Specific Language (DSL) to define configuration "recipes" and system dependencies.

- Follows a client-server architecture.

- It is highly customizable and powerful for complex infrastructure builds.

Each of these tools supports version control, role-based access, centralized logging, and auditing—making them ideal for ensuring consistent and secure deployments.

Key Benefits of Configuration Management

Automated Device Provisioning

- Streamlines initial setup and mass deployment of routers, switches, firewalls, and servers

- Reduces human error and speeds up infrastructure expansion or refresh projects

Configuration Consistency and Drift Prevention

- Ensures that every device adheres to the approved standard configurations

- Detects and corrects unauthorized or unintended changes to configuration files

Policy Enforcement and Compliance

- Automatically applies security baselines (e.g., disabling unused ports, enforcing password policies)

- Supports audit trails and compliance reporting for regulatory standards like HIPAA, PCI-DSS, and NIST 800-53

Version Control and Rollback

- Maintains historical records of configuration changes

- Allows easy rollback to a previous well-good state in case of a failed change or outage

Best Practices

Maintain Configuration Backups.

- Always keep secure, versioned backups of both baseline templates and the most recent configurations.

- Backups support recovery, auditing, and troubleshooting.

Validate Before Deployment.

- Test templates and playbooks in a sandbox or lab environment before pushing to production.

- Catch syntax errors, logic flaws, or compatibility issues early.

Use Role-Based Access Controls (RBAC).

- Protect configuration tools and store credentials by restricting who can view or modify specific device settings. Use secrets vault or password manager for credentials instead of embedding them in plaintext files.

- Integrate with centralized identity systems (e.g., LDAP, RADIUS) for consistent authentication.

Document Automation Workflows.

- Clearly describe what each playbook or script does, its prerequisites, and rollback steps.

- Ensures continuity when personnel changes occur or multiple teams manage automation tasks.

Exam Tip #25

Know the value of configuration management and recognize common tools like Ansible, Puppet, and Chef. These tools may be referenced on the exam in the context of automation or operational efficiency.

Chapter Summary

This chapter focused on the essential operational frameworks that enable modern networks to be reliable, secure, and responsive to business demands. In real-world IT environments, a strong foundation in **network operations** is what keeps mission-critical services running, supports scalability, and minimizes risk.

We began with the critical importance of **network documentation** practices, which are often underestimated but vital to effective network administration. You learned how detailed documentation, including **physical and logical diagrams**, **IP address management (IPAM)** tools, **device inventories**, and **configuration archives**, helps streamline troubleshooting, onboarding, audits, maintenance, and capacity planning. Without it, even routine tasks can become high-risk operations.

We then covered the structured and process-driven approach of **change management**, highlighting the life cycle of a change from request through post-implementation review. You saw how well-managed changes reduce risk, prevent service disruptions, and ensure accountability. We distinguished between **standard**, **emergency**, and **major** changes, emphasizing that each type requires tailored processes based on its impact, urgency, and risk level. The chapter then transitioned to **disaster recovery planning**, where you studied how organizations prepare for and recover from unexpected events such as hardware failure, cyberattacks, and natural disasters. You learned to identify critical systems using a **Business Impact Analysis (BIA)**, evaluate threats through **risk assessment**, and define acceptable downtime (**RTO**) and data loss windows (**RPO**). We examined backup strategies, site redundancy options like **hot**, **warm**, and **cold sites**, and the importance of testing and staff training.

We explored **network monitoring**, an operational necessity for proactive performance management and fault detection. Tools like **SNMP**, **Syslog**, **NetFlow**, and **packet analyzers** allow administrators to collect and analyze data across devices and layers. You learned how metrics like **latency**, **jitter**, **packet loss**, **throughput**, and **bandwidth utilization** are tracked and how baseline performance data enables faster diagnosis and future planning. Our deep dive into **fault tolerance and high availability** technologies outlined how organizations prevent downtime and maintain service continuity. This included techniques like **hardware redundancy**, **link aggregation**, **load balancing**, **failover systems**, **UPS protection**, and **server clustering**. We also covered **Service Level Agreements (SLAs)** and how they formalize uptime expectations and performance standards between clients and providers.

Finally, we examined **configuration management tools** such as **Ansible**, **Puppet**, and **Chef**. These platforms automate configuration deployment, enforce consistency across devices, maintain version control, and support compliance with organizational policies. They also reduce human error and allow rapid scaling of network infrastructure. Together, these disciplines and tools empower network professionals to operate resilient, high-performance environments that are secure, scalable, and aligned with business priorities.

Key Takeaways

Network Documentation

- Maintain accurate physical and logical network diagrams.

- Use IPAM tools to track address assignments, subnets, and DHCP scopes.

- Keep up-to-date device inventories and configuration records for compliance and recovery.

Change Management

- Follow structured workflows that include request submission, review, testing, implementation, and documentation.

- Understand the differences between standard, emergency, and major change types.

- Communicate changes to stakeholders and maintain rollback plans.

Disaster Recovery

- Use Business Impact Analysis (BIA) and risk assessments to prioritize systems.

- Define Recovery Time Objectives (RTO) and Recovery Point Objectives (RPO) based on business needs.

- Implement backup strategies and designate hot, warm, or cold recovery sites.

- Test recovery procedures and train personnel regularly.

Network Monitoring

- Use SNMP for polling device metrics and Syslog for event logging.

- Analyze traffic patterns using NetFlow/sFlow and diagnose issues with packet analyzers.

- Monitor key metrics like latency, jitter, packet loss, bandwidth, and throughput.

- Establish performance baselines and configure intelligent alerts.

High Availability and Fault Tolerance

- Design for redundancy at every level—power, hardware, links, and services.

- Use failover systems and clustering to maintain continuity.

- Employ load balancing to distribute traffic and improve performance.

- Ensure SLAs define uptime targets and support commitments with service providers.

Configuration Management

- Automate device provisioning and policy enforcement with tools like Ansible, Puppet, and Chef.

- Prevent configuration drift and support rollback with version-controlled templates.

- Validate changes before deployment and restrict tool access using RBAC.

CHAPTER 5

Network Security

In today's interconnected world, network security is no longer an optionality, it is essential. As organizations rely more heavily on digital infrastructure, their exposure to cyber threats increases. From data breaches and denial-of-service attacks to insider threats and misconfigured devices, the security landscape is vast and ever-evolving. A single weakness in a firewall rule, outdated firmware, or poorly managed access control policy can provide an entry point for malicious actors.

Understanding the nature of these threats is the foundation of a robust defense strategy. Threats can originate externally, such as from hackers, cybercriminal groups, or nation-state actors, or internally from disgruntled employees, careless users, or compromised accounts. Meanwhile, vulnerabilities may exist in software, hardware, physical infrastructure, or operational procedures—and attackers are constantly scanning for them.

Network security is not just about firewalls and antivirus software. It encompasses a comprehensive framework of tools, techniques, policies, and user awareness initiatives that together protect the confidentiality, integrity, and availability (CIA) of information systems. Professionals in this field must understand not only how attacks occur but also how to detect, respond to, and recover from them.

This chapter explores the fundamental principles of network security, including threat types, vulnerability management, security devices and technologies, authentication mechanisms, and layered defense strategies.

© Kodi A. Cochran 2026
K. A. Cochran, *CompTIA Network+ (N10-009) Certification Companion,*
Certification Study Companion Series, https://doi.org/10.1007/979-8-8688-2341-1_5

You'll also review best practices for securing wireless networks, implementing access controls, and aligning security operations with compliance and policy standards.

In this chapter, you will

- Identify common threat types and the vulnerabilities they exploit

- Learn about security hardware and software solutions used to defend networks

- Understand authentication, authorization, and accounting (AAA) principles

- Explore methods for securing wireless networks and remote access

- Review best practices for implementing defense-in-depth strategies

- Examine policy-based approaches to risk mitigation and compliance

By mastering these topics, you'll be equipped to design, deploy, and manage secure network environments—and be well-prepared for the security-focused objectives of the CompTIA Network+ exam.

Types of Threats and Common Vulnerabilities

Before you can defend a network, you need to understand what you're up against. Threats come in many forms—some technical, some human—but all of them can disrupt operations, steal data, or damage systems if the right defenses aren't in place. And while external attackers are a serious concern, internal threats and misconfigurations often pose just as much risk.

At the basic level: a threat is anything with the potential to cause harm (an attacker, malware, or even a disaster); a vulnerability is a weakness that can be exploited; and risk is the likelihood and impact if that exploitation happens. Security work is ultimately risk management—reducing exposure, limiting impact, and making successful attacks harder.

Common vectors include malware, phishing and other social engineering, unpatched software, weak configurations, and physical tampering. Some attacks are opportunistic; others are long-running campaigns (APTs) that move quietly and deliberately.

Common Threat Types

- **Malware:**
  - Short for malicious software, malware includes viruses, worms, trojans, ransomware, and spyware.
  - It can destroy data, hijack system resources, spy on user activity, or lock files and demand payment.

- **Rootkits:**
  - Often delivered through email attachments, compromised websites, or infected removable drives.

- **Phishing:**
  - A form of social engineering where attackers pose as trusted contacts to trick users into revealing sensitive information.
  - Often sent through fake emails, login pages, or text messages.

- Targets credentials, banking info, or access to internal systems.

- **Man-in-the-Middle (MitM):**

  - An attacker intercepts communications between two parties—often without either party realizing it.

  - Can allow data theft or session hijacking.

  - Especially common on unsecured public Wi-Fi if HTTPS or VPN protections aren't in place.

- **Denial of Service (DoS)/Distributed DoS (DDoS):**

  - DoS attacks flood a system or service with requests until it crashes or becomes unresponsive.

  - DDoS takes it further by using a network of compromised devices (botnet) to launch the attack from multiple sources, making it harder to block.

- **Insider Threats:**

  - These originate from people within the organization—employees, contractors, or vendors—who have access to systems or data.

  - May be intentional (sabotage or theft) or accidental (misuse, poor security hygiene).

  - It is harder to detect because insiders often have legitimate access.

Common Vulnerabilities

Threats exploit vulnerabilities—weak points in systems, configurations, or behavior. Some are technical; others are procedural.

- **Unpatched Software:**

  - Outdated operating systems, applications, or firmware are frequent targets.

  - Attackers routinely scan for systems running with known CVEs (Common Vulnerabilities and Exposures).

- **Misconfigurations:**

  - Open ports, weak passwords, disabled firewalls, and over-permissioned accounts are all low-hanging fruit.

  - Common in default setups or when systems are rushed into production.

- **Lack of Encryption:**

  - Data sent without encryption can be intercepted and read—especially over wireless or public networks.

  - Applies to both data in transit and data at rest.

- **Default Credentials:**

  - Devices or software installed with factory usernames and passwords are easy for attackers to find and exploit.

  - IoT devices and admin interfaces are common culprits.

Best Practices for Reducing Risk

- **Run Regular Vulnerability Assessments and Pen Tests:**
    - Identify weak spots before attackers do.
    - Tools like Nessus or OpenVAS can help automate scanning.

- **Patch Systems Promptly:**
    - Stay on top of security updates for operating systems, applications, and firmware.
    - Prioritize critical CVEs in production environments.

- **Train Your Users:**
    - Many breaches start with human error. Train staff on phishing recognition, safe browsing, and incident reporting.

- **Apply Least Privilege Principles:**
    - Give users only the access they need—nothing more.
    - Reduces the blast radius if an account is compromised.

Exam Tip #26

Expect questions that ask you to match a threat (e.g., phishing, MitM, ransomware) to its description or identify which vulnerability it exploits. Scenario questions may also ask how to reduce risk through patching, encryption, or access controls.

Authentication, Authorization, and Accounting (AAA)

AAA is a foundational concept in network security. It defines how access is controlled, how users are identified, and how activity is logged. Together, these three components ensure that users are who they claim to be, that they can only access what they're authorized to, and that all actions are tracked for auditing and compliance.

- **Authentication**: Verifies identity. This typically involves usernames and passwords, but can also include certificates, biometrics, tokens, or multi-factor authentication (MFA).

- **Authorization**: Grants access based on permissions. After a user is authenticated, the system checks what they're allowed to do.

- **Accounting**: Logs the activity of users. Tracks login times, session durations, accessed resources, and actions performed.

Real-World Example

A company uses a RADIUS server to handle remote access authentication for VPN users. Employees log in using a username/password and verify their identity with a mobile MFA app. Once connected, role-based rules restrict access—IT staff can access internal servers, while regular users are limited to general tools. Every session is logged centrally, including login times, source IPs, and duration, for security monitoring and auditing.

Access Control Models

Access control is about deciding who gets access to what—and under what conditions. There are several models used depending on the organization's needs, security policies, and regulatory requirements.

Role-Based Access Control (RBAC):

- Access is granted based on the user's role in the organization.

- Allots roles to group users with similar responsibilities (e.g., HR, Finance, IT).

- Easier to manage at scale—changing a role's permissions affects all users in that role.

Attribute-Based Access Control (ABAC):

- More dynamic and granular than RBAC.

- Access is based on a combination of attributes—such as user role, location, time of day, data sensitivity, and device health.

- Allows fine-grained policy enforcement but is more complex to manage.

Access Control Lists (ACLs):

- Specify which users or systems can access a particular object (e.g., file, folder, device) and what actions they can perform (read, write, execute).

- Applied to network devices, operating systems, and file systems.

Real-World Example

At a university, professors can access and modify student coursework, while staff in the registrar's office can update tuition billing but cannot view grades. Access is granted via RBAC. Meanwhile, network file servers enforce ACLs at the file system level to control who can view or edit sensitive documents.

RBAC vs. ABAC Comparison Table

	RBAC	ABAC
Basis	User's assigned role	Attributes (user, environment, object, action)
Flexibility	Moderate	High
Granularity	Role/group-level	Policy-based, condition-driven
Example	Sales role = access to CRM	Grant access if role = Sales AND location = HQ

Security Devices and Technologies: IDS vs. IPS

	IDS (Intrusion Detection System)	IPS (Intrusion Prevention System)
Primary role	Detects suspicious traffic and alerts	Detects and actively blocks threats
Traffic flow	Passive (out-of-band monitoring)	Inline (actively processes all traffic)

(continued)

	IDS (Intrusion Detection System)	IPS (Intrusion Prevention System)
Latency risk	Low (does not interfere with traffic)	Higher (may introduce delay depending on load)
Use case	Alert on unusual traffic or anomalies	Stop DDoS attacks, malware, or unauthorized access

Key Point:

IDS is good for visibility and forensic analysis. IPS is used when immediate threat-blocking is required, especially in environments with strict availability and security requirements.

1. Use a centralized SIEM (Security Information and Event Management) tool for correlation and alerting.

2. Regularly validate against benchmarks like CIS (Center for Internet Security) or DISA STIGs.

Secure Protocols and Their Functions

Encrypting data in transit protects against eavesdropping, tampering, and spoofing. Below are common security protocols and their primary uses:

HTTPS (Hypertext Transfer Protocol Secure):

- Encrypts web traffic using SSL/TLS

- Protects login forms, transactions, and session data on websites

SSH (Secure Shell):

- Secures remote access to systems via encrypted command-line sessions

- Commonly used to manage routers, switches, Linux servers, and cloud systems

SFTP (SSH File Transfer Protocol):

- Uses SSH for secure file transfer and directory operations

- Encrypted alternative to standard FTP

FTPS (FTP Secure):

- Adds SSL/TLS encryption to legacy FTP

- Less common than SFTP but still in use in some enterprise systems

IPSec (Internet Protocol Security):

- Encrypts and authenticates IP packets

- Used for VPNs (both site-to-site and client-to-site), often with ESP or AH protocols

TLS (Transport Layer Security):

- Secures various protocols, including HTTPS, VoIP (SIP), SMTP (email), and IMAP

- Replaces SSL in modern cryptographic implementations

DNSSEC (Domain Name System Security Extensions):

- Adds integrity and origin authentication to DNS responses

- Prevents DNS spoofing and cache poisoning attacks

Secure Protocol Best Practices

Disable Insecure Protocols:

- Avoid Telnet, FTP, and HTTP in production environments. Use their secure counterparts (SSH, SFTP, HTTPS).

Enforce Current TLS Versions:

- Disable TLS 1.0 and 1.1, which are considered insecure. Require TLS 1.2 or 1.3.

Use Trusted Certificate Authorities (CAs):

- Only install certificates signed by recognized and secure authorities.

- Self-sign certificates should be limited to internal use and properly distributed.

Validate Configurations During Hardening:

- Routinely audit protocol settings across network devices, servers, and endpoints to ensure best practices are enforced.

Exam Tip #27

Be ready to identify secure protocols by their function (e.g., remote admin, file transfer, VPN tunneling). Know the differences between SFTP and FTPS and understand when to use IPSec vs. TLS. You may also see questions involving outdated protocol usage and how to replace them.

Physical Security and Environmental Controls

While firewalls and encryption protect data from digital threats, physical security defends against tampering, theft, and destruction of the hardware that powers the network. Without proper physical and environmental controls, even the most secure networks are vulnerable. Attackers don't always need to crack a password—sometimes all they need is a way into the server room.

This section focuses on securing physical infrastructure such as wiring closets, server racks, and data centers, as well as maintaining environmental conditions to prevent damage or service interruptions.

Physical Security Controls

Access Control Systems:

- Control who can physically enter secure areas like server rooms or data centers.

- Use badge readers, biometric scanners (fingerprint, retina), PIN pads, or smart cards.

- Often integrated with centralized logging systems to track access history.

Surveillance (CCTV):

- Cameras placed at entry points and sensitive areas to monitor activity and deter unauthorized access.

- Footage can be used for auditing, incident investigation, and compliance.

Locking Cabinets and Racks:

- Individual equipment enclosures can be secured to prevent unauthorized users from accessing switches, servers, or patch panels—even if they gain room access.

Mantraps:

- Two-door entry systems that allow only one person to pass through at a time.

- Helps prevent tailgating (when an unauthorized person follows an authorized person into a secure area).

Security Guards:

- Provide a human layer of protection

- Can intervene in real time, enforce policy, and verify identity during access attempts

Environmental Controls

HVAC Systems (Heating, Ventilation, and Air Conditioning):

- Regulate temperature and humidity in server rooms and data centers.

    1. In larger facilities, hot/cold aisle containment is used to control airflow and improve cooling efficiency.

- Excess heat can shorten equipment lifespan or cause spontaneous shutdowns.

- Proper airflow and climate control are essential for system reliability.

Fire Detection and Suppression: Wet-pipe sprinklers are common in general office spaces, but dry-pipe or pre-action systems are often preferred in server rooms because they reduce the chance of accidental discharge onto electronics.

- Systems include smoke detectors, alarms, and suppression agents

- Common suppression methods:

  1. FM-200: Clean agent that extinguishes fire without damaging electronics.

  2. Inert Gas Systems (e.g., Argonite): Reduce oxygen levels to suppress combustion.

- Sprinkler-based systems are still in use but can damage electronics if triggered.

Uninterruptible Power Supplies (UPS):

- Provide temporary power during short outages or fluctuations. This is battery-backed power meant to bridge short outages and support controlled shutdown or failover.

- Allow graceful shutdown or failover to backup systems to prevent data loss and corruption.

- Often combined with surge protection.

Backup Generators:

- Supply power for extended outages

- Typically fueled by diesel or natural gas

- Automatically activate after detecting a loss of utility power, often within seconds

Best Practices

Restrict Physical Access:

- Only authorized personnel should be allowed into secure facilities or access to hardware.

- Review access logs and permissions periodically.

Perform Routine Inspections:

- Regularly inspect locks, doors, power systems, and HVAC equipment to identify failures or tampering.

Integrate Environmental Sensors:

- Use temperature, humidity, smoke, and water sensors connected to monitoring systems for early warning.

- Set alerts to trigger automatic notifications or shutdowns if thresholds are exceeded.

Include Physical Security in Risk Assessments:

- Don't separate physical and cybersecurity. Both should be evaluated in risk audits and incident response planning.

Exam Tip #28

Be ready to identify physical security components like mantraps, surveillance, and badge systems—and pair them with their use cases. Expect scenarios that require you to recommend environmental controls such as HVAC or UPS for data center protection.

Network Hardening Techniques

Network hardening is about locking down systems by eliminating unnecessary exposure. Every extra service running, every open port, and every unused feature adds to the attack surface. Reducing that surface makes it harder for attackers to gain a foothold—and easier for defenders to monitor what matters.

Hardening is not a one-time task—it's a life cycle process. Devices should be hardened before deployment and regularly reviewed afterward, especially when new software or patches are introduced. Use host-based firewalls and network ACLs to block unwanted traffic at the source.

Common Network Hardening Techniques

Unused Services and Ports:

- Turn off default services and protocols that aren't required for operation.

- Use host-based firewalls and network ACLs to block unwanted traffic at the source. Examples include Windows Defender Firewall on Windows and iptables/nftables on Linux.

Default Credentials:

- Change factory-set usernames and passwords immediately after deployment.

- Use complex, unique credentials for each system—ideally combined with MFA.

Apply Security Patches Promptly:

- Keep OS, applications, drivers, and firmware current.

- Use automated patch management platforms to enforce consistency across endpoints.

Limit Administrative Access:

- Admin privileges should only be assigned to those who absolutely need them.

- Implement the principle of least privilege (PoLP).

- Require MFA for all privileged accounts and remote access sessions.

Enable Logging and Auditing:

- Configure system logs to track authentication attempts, configuration changes, and resource usage.

- Use a centralized SIEM (Security Information and Event Management) tool for correlation and alerting. Common examples include Splunk, Elastic/ELK, and Graylog.

MAC Address Filtering:

- Restrict access to wired or wireless networks by whitelisting authorized device MAC addresses.

- Should be layered with other controls (e.g., 802.1X), as MACs can be spoofed.

Disable Unused Interfaces:

- Physically disconnect unused Ethernet ports on switches.

- Administratively disable interfaces not in use and shut down legacy protocols like Telnet.

Hardening Best Practices

Use Configuration Baselines:

- Define and apply standardized secure configurations across all systems and devices.

- Regularly validate against benchmarks like CIS (Center for Internet Security) or DISA STIGs. SCAP-compliant assessment tools can also help automate validation on a scale.

Test Before Rolling Out:

- Validate hardening changes in staging environments to ensure functionality isn't disrupted.

  1. Have a rollback plan ready before production changes—ideally automated—so you can quickly recover if a change breaks functionality.

Document and Monitor Changes:

- Track configuration changes with version control or change management tools.

  1. Version control often means Git, while configuration management tools (Ansible, Puppet, or similar) help enforce baselines consistently. In many environments, endpoint platforms like SCCM also play a role in standardizing settings.

- Alert on unexpected modifications or deviations from baseline.

Exam Tip #29

Hardening reduces your attack surface. Expect questions that ask which ports or services to disable, how to apply patches securely, or how to lock down access without disrupting operations.

Social Engineering and User Awareness

The strongest firewall can't stop someone from clicking a fake invoice or giving up their password to a convincing voice on the phone. Social engineering is the art of exploiting human behavior to bypass technical controls, and it's one of the most common—and successful—attack methods.

Whether it's phishing emails, fake tech support calls, or someone slipping through the door behind a badge holder, human error remains a leading cause of security breaches. That's why user awareness is just as critical as technical defense.

Common Social Engineering Techniques

Phishing:

- Deceptive messages (usually email) that appear to come from trusted sources. Phishing frequently relies on spoofed or lookalike domains and fake portals to feel legitimate.

- Typically try to trick users into clicking malicious links, downloading malware, or entering credentials into fake login pages.

Spear Phishing:

- A more targeted form of phishing that uses personal details about the recipient to build trust.

- May reference recent purchases, job titles, or known contacts.

  1. `That personalization usually comes from OSINT (open-source intelligence)—public data, social media, data brokers, or details leaked in previous breaches that attackers stitch together to sound credible.

Vishing and Smishing: These often use caller ID spoofing to increase trust and urgency.

- Vishing (voice phishing): Phone-based scams pretending to be banks, IT support, or government agencies

- Smishing (SMS phishing): Fraudulent text messages containing links or requests for information

Tailgating:

- An attacker physically follows an authorized person into a secure area without proper authentication.

- Common in offices without mantraps or enforced badge checks.

Pretexting:

- The attacker fabricates a story or identity to gain trust and extract information.

- Often used in desk scams or vendor impersonation attempts.

Impersonation:

- Pretending to be a trusted figure—such as IT staff or an executive—to trick users into handing over access or credentials.

User Awareness Strategies

Security Awareness Training:

Conduct regular, mandatory sessions on phishing recognition, password security, and incident reporting. Quarterly training is a solid baseline, and shorter "micro-trainings" between sessions help keep it fresh. Adaptive or gamified platforms can improve engagement without turning training into a checkbox.

For example, finance leaders (like a CFO) are common targets for business email compromise (BEC), while IT teams often see helpdesk impersonation and "urgent password reset" scams. Track metrics like click-through rate, credential submission attempts, and (most importantly) reporting rate. Use that data to tune the training and focus on the teams or workflows that keep getting targeted.

Phishing Simulations:

- Send fake phishing messages to test employees' readiness and highlight areas for improvement.

Encourage a "Stop and Verify" Culture:

- Teach users to question unusual requests—even if they appear to come from inside the organization.

- Provide easy, non-punitive ways to report suspicious messages or behavior.

Physical Security Reinforcement:

- Use signage to deter tailgating and train staff to challenge unfamiliar individuals in restricted areas.

Social Engineering Best Practices

Reinforce Policies with Training:

- Tie user education to company policies on data handling, access controls, and acceptable use.

    1. When possible, tailor training towards policy acknowledgment, so sign-offs are tracked and auditable.

Hold People Accountable:

Reward good security behavior and address repeated lapses through coaching and escalation. Some organizations even include security behaviors in performance reviews or use lightweight recognition (like friendly leaderboards) to reinforce good habits.

Make Reporting Easy:

Create simple channels (e.g., email, button in Outlook, hotline) for employees to report phishing or suspected attacks.

Exam Tip #30

Social engineering doesn't target systems, it targets people. Expect scenario questions that ask how to recognize or mitigate phishing, impersonation, or tailgating. Be prepared to identify effective user training practices.

Chapter Summary

In this chapter, you explored the core principles of network security domain that spans far beyond just firewalls and antivirus software. Securing a network today requires layered defenses across infrastructure, users, devices, and physical spaces.

We started by breaking down common threats and vulnerabilities, including malware, phishing attacks, man-in-the-middle exploits, denial-of-service attempts, and insider threats. You learned how attackers exploit weak points like unpatched systems, misconfigured access, and default credentials. From there, we discussed key mitigation strategies: regular updates, user training, principle of least privilege, and vulnerability assessments. Next, you reviewed the AAA model—Authentication, Authorization, and Accounting, which forms the foundation for identity and access control. You saw how authentication verifies user identity, authorization enforces role-based permissions, and accounting tracks system access for auditing and compliance.

We then examined access control models, including Discretionary (DAC), Mandatory (MAC), Role-Based (RBAC), and Attribute-Based (ABAC). Each model serves a different purpose depending on how granular and flexible access needs to be. Real-world examples helped illustrate how these models apply in environments like universities, enterprises, and government systems. The chapter then covered essential security devices and technologies, including firewalls, IDS/IPS systems, VPN concentrators, proxy servers, and SIEM platforms. You learned the difference between detection and prevention, inline vs. out-of-band monitoring, and how centralized logging supports incident response.

We explored secure communication protocols, including HTTPS, SSH, IPSec, TLS, and DNSSEC. You reviewed the differences between secure file transfer methods (SFTP vs. FTPS) and the role of certificates and encryption in protecting data in transit. You also reviewed best practices for disabling insecure protocols and enforcing current cryptographic standards. Beyond technical defenses, we discussed physical security and environmental controls—critical yet often overlooked areas. You learned about access controls (badges, mantraps, surveillance), environmental systems (HVAC, fire suppression, UPS), and the importance of aligning physical protection with digital security policies.

You were also introduced to network hardening techniques, which reduce the attack surface by removing unnecessary services, disabling unused ports, enforcing strong authentication, and applying strict configuration baselines. These practices are essential in securing routers, switches, firewalls, and servers from compromise. Finally, we addressed the human factor through social engineering and user awareness. You explored how phishing, vishing, tailgating, and impersonation exploit human trust rather than system flaws—and how user education, training simulations, and strong security culture can mitigate these risks.

Taken together, these security layers—technical, physical, procedural, and human—form a resilient defense strategy. As a network professional, your job isn't just to respond to threats but to anticipate them, reduce risk, and build systems that can withstand attack.

Key Takeaways

1. **Threats and Vulnerabilities:**

   - Understand the differences between threat types (e.g., malware, phishing, insider threats) and vulnerabilities (e.g., unpatched systems, misconfigurations).

   - Recognize how attackers exploit these gaps and how to reduce risk through updates, access control, and user training.

2. **AAA (Authentication, Authorization, Accounting):**

   - Authentication verifies identity using credentials or MFA.

   - Authorization defines what users can access based on roles or policies.

- Accounting logs access and use for auditing and incident response.

3. **Access Control Models:**

   - DAC (Discretionary): Resource owner controls access.

   - MAC (Mandatory): Enforced by system policies and classifications.

   - RBAC (Role-Based): Access tied to user roles.

   - ABAC (Attribute-Based): Access based on multiple attributes (role, time, location, etc.).

4. **Security Devices and Technologies:**

   - Firewalls control traffic flow at the network edge or host level.

   - IDS/IPS detect and respond to suspicious traffic.

   - Proxy servers and VPN concentrators secure communications and enforce policy.

   - SIEM platforms aggregate logs and support threat detection and compliance.

5. **Secure Protocols:**

   - Use HTTPS, SSH, SFTP, IPSec, TLS, and DNSSEC to encrypt data in transit.

   - Know the differences between SFTP and FTPS.

   - Disable insecure protocols like Telnet, FTP, and older SSL/TLS versions.

6. **Physical Security and Environmental Controls**:

   - Secure equipment using badge readers, mantraps, surveillance, and locking racks.

   - Maintain safe operating conditions with HVAC, fire suppression, UPS, and generators.

   - Include physical security in overall risk assessments.

7. **Network Hardening:**

   - Disable unused ports and services.

   - Remove default credentials and enforce strong authentication.

   - Apply security patches consistently and use configuration baselines.

   - Enable logging and monitor changes for unauthorized activity.

8. **Social Engineering and User Awareness:**

   - Recognize phishing, vishing, tailgating, pretexting, and impersonation attacks.

   - Train users regularly and simulate attacks to test readiness.

   - Promote a culture where security is everyone's responsibility.

CHAPTER 6

Network Troubleshooting

Even the most well-designed and carefully managed network will eventually experience issues. Whether it's a user unable to connect to the Internet, a misconfigured device causing latency, or a deeper infrastructure failure—problems will arise. What separates a competent technician from a highly valued network professional is the ability to troubleshoot those problems efficiently, calmly, and systematically.

In this chapter, we're going to focus on what really matters: resolving problems with clarity and control. You'll learn a structured approach to troubleshooting that's grounded in real-world experience—not guesswork. We'll walk through the industry-recognized troubleshooting methodology, break down each stage into practical actions, and tie it back to common issues you'll encounter in the field.

We'll also cover the tools you'll need to do the job right—from protocol analyzers and cable testers to command-line diagnostics like ping, tracert, and netstat. You'll learn what tools to use, when to use them, and what information to expect. More importantly, you'll understand how to interpret those results and take action that leads to resolution.

Troubleshooting is not just a technical skill—it's a mindset. It requires patience, a clear head under pressure, and a commitment to understanding the root cause of an issue, not just masking the symptoms.

© Kodi A. Cochran 2026

K. A. Cochran, *CompTIA Network+ (N10-009) Certification Companion,*
Certification Study Companion Series, https://doi.org/10.1007/979-8-8688-2341-1_6

We'll cover how to spot patterns that may indicate deeper systemic issues, how to separate user error from infrastructure failure, and how to document findings in a way that supports continuous improvement.

By the end of this chapter, you'll be equipped with practical knowledge and confidence to respond to network anomalies, outages, and degraded performance—across both wired and wireless environments, in small offices or complex enterprise environments. This isn't just theory. This is what you need when the ticket comes in and users are already frustrated.

Let's get into it.

Structured Troubleshooting Methodology

Troubleshooting without a plan leads to wasted time, confusion, and repeated mistakes. In a live environment, that's not acceptable—downtime impacts business operations and user trust. A structured, repeatable methodology keeps you focused, speeds up resolution, and helps others follow your work. Whether you're working solo or part of a larger IT team, following this approach ensures consistency and professionalism.

The CompTIA Network+ exam emphasizes a **six-step troubleshooting model**—and it's one that you'll use often in your career. Below is each step, along with practical insight into how to apply it effectively.

Note   Always begin troubleshooting at the physical layer (Layer 1); a "no Internet" problem could stem from Layer 7 (DNS timeouts), Layer 3 (DHCP failures), or a disconnected cable.

Identify the Problem

Start by gathering **complete and accurate information**. Jumping to conclusions is a common mistake—slow down and observe.

- **Talk to the user**: Ask clear, open-ended questions: *"When did it start?" "What changed?" "Is it just you or others too?"*

- **Check logs and alerts**: Review logs from switches, firewalls, access points, or syslog servers, and don't forget core services (for example, DHCP logs like dhcpd.log or DHCP events in Windows Event Viewer).

- **Document affected systems or services**: Is it one machine? A VLAN? An entire subnet?

Don't overlook the basics. A "no Internet" complaint could be a DNS issue, a disconnected patch cable, or expired user credentials. **Check everything from Layer 1 (physical) to Layer 7 (application).**

Establish a Theory of Probable Cause

Once you have enough details, start developing a hypothesis.

- **Look for common causes first**: Unplugged cables, NIC failures, software patches gone bad.

- **Use known-good comparisons**: Is a nearby workstation working fine on the same switch?

- **Leverage historical knowledge**: If the issue has happened before, reuse what you've learned.

Don't be afraid to say, *"I'm not sure yet."* Good troubleshooting isn't about speed—it's about accuracy.

Test the Theory

Now it's time to **validate your assumption**.

- Use command-line tools like ping, tracert, ipconfig, nslookup, dig, netstat, arp -a, and telnet to verify connectivity, name resolution, and basic session behavior.

- Change one variable at a time—test with a new cable, move to a different port, try a different DNS server.

- Use isolation—Does the problem occur on a different network? From a different device?

If your test proves the theory wrong, **don't force it**—go back to Step 2 and re-evaluate. Never treat assumptions as facts.

Establish a Plan of Action and Implement the Solution

Once you're confident in your diagnosis, prepare a fix.

1. **Minimize disruption**: If the change affects production, schedule it accordingly.

2. **Communicate early**: Let stakeholders know what you're changing and why.

3. **Have a rollback plan**: If the fix fails, you need to recover quickly.

Never make changes directly to production systems without a plan. Even the right fix can go wrong if done impulsively.

Verify Full System Functionality

After implementing the fix, **validate that everything works**—not just the issue at hand. Review relevant logs and confirm monitoring alerts have cleared. Validate with multiple affected users (and a quick spot-check of adjacent services) before closing the ticket.

1. Is the issue resolved for all affected users?

2. Have any services been unintentionally disrupted?

3. Are monitoring alerts clear and system logs clean?

Ask for user confirmation, and if needed, continue to monitor over the next few hours or days. **Don't mark the ticket as closed until you're sure.**

Document Findings, Actions, and Outcomes

This is where many techs cut corners—don't be one of them. Documentation protects you, your team, and your network.

1. Record exactly what the issue was, what you tried, what worked, and why.

2. Update any internal documentation, including SOPs or known-issue trackers.

3. If this was the result of a change gone wrong, link it back to your change management system and reference the related change request ID. If it was an outage or user impact, include the incident/ticket ID as well.

Clear documentation prevents repeat mistakes and improves resolution times in the future. It also shows that you take your role seriously.

Best Practices for Network Troubleshooting

- **Communicate openly** with users and managers during outages.

- **Always follow the steps—even under pressure.**

- **Don't rush to replace equipment**—test before buying new gear.

- **Correlate logs and monitoring tools** to pinpoint intermittent issues.

- **Treat every issue as a chance to learn and improve.**

Exam Tip #31

Memorize the six steps of the troubleshooting model in order:

1. Identify the problem.

2. Establish a theory of probable cause.

3. Test the theory.

4. Establish a plan of action and implement the solution.

5. Verify full system functionality.

6. Document findings, actions, and outcomes.

CompTIA often asks you to determine what step you're in or what action should come next. Practice applying the model to real-world scenarios.

Common Network Issues

Understanding common network issues is critical for quickly identifying symptoms and applying the right troubleshooting process. These problems can occur at any layer of the OSI model—and the key to resolving them is knowing where to start. In the field, your ability to match symptoms to causes will often determine how fast you can restore service.

Let's break down frequent issues by layer, including wireless-specific problems and cross-layer patterns you should watch for.

Physical Layer Issues

At Layer 1, connectivity is binary—it either works or it doesn't. Always start by verifying cables, power, and physical connections.

1. **Cable faults or disconnections** can cause total loss of signal or sporadic connectivity.

2. **Damaged connectors or ports** may result in intermittent link drops or signal degradation.

3. **Power supply failures** in access points or switches can silently bring down entire segments, especially with PoE (Power over Ethernet) devices.

Real-World Example

A user reports their VoIP phone suddenly stopped working. After basic troubleshooting, you find the copper pins inside the wall jack are bent, and the PoE switch isn't delivering power. Re-terminating the jack restores full functionality.

Data Link Layer Issues

Layer 2 handles frame transmission between directly connected nodes—when it fails, you'll often see strange local issues.

1. MAC address conflicts can occur when duplicate MAC addresses (or spoofed MACs) confuse switches and misdirect traffic.

2. **Switch port errors** like CRC mismatches or collisions usually indicate physical issues or misconfigured interfaces.

3. **Duplex mismatches** (half vs. full) lead to low throughput and dropped packets—especially during large transfers.

Network Layer Issues

Routing and logical addressing live at Layer 3. If devices can't communicate beyond their local network, this layer is often to blame.

1. **Incorrect IP addresses or subnet masks** prevent proper routing and device discovery.

2. **Default gateway misconfigurations** stop outbound traffic from reaching its destination.

3. **DNS resolution failures** impact users even when the network is otherwise healthy.

Application Layer Issues

When lower layers are working fine, the root cause may lie in the configuration of services and applications at Layer 7.

1. **DHCP misconfiguration** (e.g., exhausted scopes) can result in IP conflicts or connectivity delays.

2. **Authentication server downtime** (e.g., RADIUS, LDAP, AD) can block logins or resource access.

3. **Firewall rules** may accidentally block required ports or protocols, disrupting legitimate traffic.

Wireless-Specific Issues

Wireless networking introduces unique variables that wired connections avoid.

1. Signal interference from microwaves, wireless phones, or thick walls can kill performance. Co-channel and adjacent-channel interference (often from multiple nearby APs on overlapping channels) can produce the same symptoms, especially in crowded 2.4 GHz environments.

2. **Incorrect SSID or security keys** will stop client devices from joining altogether.

3. **Channel overlaps** in dense environments like offices or apartments lead to packet collisions and slower speeds.

Cross-Layer Symptoms to Watch For

Some issues span multiple OSI layers or appear in hard-to-pinpoint ways. Here's what to keep an eye on:

1. **Intermittent connectivity**: Often caused by faulty cables, loose connections, or wireless interference

2. **Slow network performance**: Could be high bandwidth usage, jitter, excessive retransmissions, or misconfigured QoS

3. **Inability to access specific hosts**: May stem from bad DNS records, ACLs, or incorrect static routes

4. **Duplicate IP address alerts**: Result from static IP conflicts or mismanaged DHCP environments

5. **Authentication timeouts**: Often due to expired certificates, overloaded servers, or dropped RADIUS/TACACS+ packets

Best Practices

1. **Start at the lowest possible OSI layer** and work your way up—physical issues are more common than many assume.

2. **Replicate the issue when it's safe** to do so—this is especially important for software or policy-related problems.

3. **Use logs, timestamps, and monitoring tools** to correlate user reports with system activity.

4. **Document the scope clearly**: Who is affected, how often it happens, and what symptoms are present.

Exam Tip #32

Be able to **match symptoms with likely causes**. For example, if users report slow performance only on Wi-Fi connections, investigate signal interference, client density, or bandwidth restrictions. If one subnet can't reach another, consider gateway or VLAN misconfigurations.

Troubleshooting Tools

When it comes to solving network issues, having the right tools makes all the difference. Tools serve one key purpose: to help you **verify assumptions with data**. Whether you're in the field with physical gear or at a console running diagnostics, choosing the right tool for the situation is what separates guesswork from effective troubleshooting. This section introduces both physical tools and command-line/software utilities, showing you when to use each—and what kind of information they provide. When documenting, including the root cause, tools and tests used, final resolution, and any updates to standard operating procedures or automation, link the documentation to the incident or change request ID.

Physical Tools

These are essential when troubleshooting physical layer problems—especially in structured cabling environments, patch panels, or unknown wiring situations.

Cable Tester

1. Detects open wires, short circuits, split pairs, and miswires.

2. Advanced models provide distance-to-fault measurements using Time-Domain Reflectometry (TDR).

Tone Generator and Probe

1.   Sends an audible tone through a cable, allowing you to trace its path.

2.   Indispensable in crowded server rooms or above-ceiling wiring—helps avoid unplugging the wrong cable.

Loopback Adapter

1.   Plugs into a port and "loops" data back to the sender

2.   Used to test NIC functionality or verify that switch ports are working as expected

Multimeter

1.   Measures voltage, continuity, and resistance

2.   Useful for verifying cable integrity, detecting broken wires, or testing power adapters

Real-World Example

During a site visit, a technician needs to identify which of several cables runs to a remote office. Instead of guessing, they attach a tone generator to one end and use the probe to accurately locate the cable behind a ceiling tile—avoiding accidental disconnection of active systems.

Software and Command-Line Tools

These tools provide visibility into how data flows across the network, how devices communicate, and where the failures occur. Use command-line tools like ping, tracert, ipconfig, nslookup, or netstat.

ping

1. Tests basic IP connectivity using ICMP echo
    requests

2. Detects packet loss, high latency, or lack of response

tracert (Windows)/traceroute (Linux/macOS)

1. Displays each hop between the local host and
    destination

2. Helps identify routing loops, dropped paths, or slow
    segments

ipconfig/ifconfig/ip

1. Shows IP address, subnet mask, gateway, and DNS
    settings

2. ipconfig/release and/renew allow manual DHCP
    operations

nslookup/dig

1. Tests DNS name resolution

2. Helps verify that hostnames are resolved correctly
    and DNS servers are reachable

netstat

1. Lists current TCP/UDP sessions and listening ports

2. Identifies abnormal open connections or listening services that shouldn't be running

arp

1. Displays MAC-to-IP address mappings in the ARP cache

2. Can help detect ARP spoofing, duplicate IPs, or unexpected MACs

nmap

1. Performs port scans, OS detection, and service identification

2. Used for both inventory audits and security analysis

Wireshark

1. A powerful packet capture and analysis tool

2. Filters by protocol, IP, port, or content to reveal precise behavior

TFTP/FTP Clients

1. Used to transfer files to and from network devices (e.g., switch configs, firmware)

2. Often required when devices lack modern file transfer protocols like SMB or HTTPS

Best Practices

1. **Match your tool to the suspected OSI layer**. Don't run traceroute when the cable might just be unplugged.

2. **Keep a record** of your findings: Timestamps, IPs, and results help you establish a clear timeline.

3. **Correlate user complaints with logs and output**: ping may show 100% success while the user experiences app failures due to DNS or port issues.

4. **Scrub sensitive data**: Especially with tools like Wireshark, avoid storing or sharing packet captures that contain usernames, passwords, or internal traffic.

Exam Tip #33

Know the **purpose, syntax, and expected output** of each tool. For example:

1. A ping timeout could indicate a firewall rule, not necessarily a downed host.

2. A tracert that fails at the third hop might point to a problematic router or blocked ICMP traffic.

3. A netstat output showing hundreds of connections on an unknown port could suggest malware.

Key Techniques and Tools

Bandwidth Testing

1. Tools like iPerf, Speedtest, and vendor-specific performance monitors measure data transfer rates.

2. Useful for validating link capacity, troubleshooting slow WAN connections, or confirming ISP performance.

3. If bandwidth looks sufficient but performance still suffers, look deeper—the issue may be on the application side or involve retransmissions.

Latency Testing

1. Latency measures the round-trip time for data to travel between two endpoints.

2. High latency can stem from long routing paths, congested links, or satellite connections.

3. Tools like ping and traceroute help measure latency and identify the hope where it increases.

Packet Loss Detection

1. Packet loss causes choppy videos, broken audio, and failed downloads.

2. It may be intermittent and hard to catch—testing over time or under load is key.

3. Use ping -n 100, pathping, or deep analysis in Wireshark to detect where packets are being dropped.

Jitter Measurement

1. Jitter is the variation in packet delay—especially disruptive to VoIP and video.

2. Even with good bandwidth, high jitter makes calls unintelligible or video jittery.

3. Monitored using QoS dashboards, VoIP monitoring tools, or specialized appliances.

Throughput Analysis

1. Throughput measures how much usable data is delivered successfully—not just bandwidth.

2. If throughput is lower than expected, look for retransmissions, duplex mismatches, or interference.

3. iPerf, SNMP-based monitors, and flow-based analytics (e.g., NetFlow) help track this.

DNS Resolution Checks

1. Slow DNS lookups feel like slow Internet—even when the connection is fine.

2. Tools like nslookup, dig, or testing with alternate DNS servers (like 8.8.8.8) help confirm whether delays stem from name resolution.

Application Layer Testing

1. Sometimes everything looks good until a user logs in or performs a task—that's where app-layer testing comes in.

2. Simulate user behavior: Log into services, submit forms, or load dashboards.

3. Tools range from scripts (e.g., cURL, Selenium) to enterprise monitoring platforms.

Real-World Example

Users report long delays with accessing cloud-based CRM, even though Internet speeds seem fine. Bandwidth tests confirm sufficient capacity, but DNS lookups for the CRM's domain are taking over 500ms. Investigation reveals misconfigured forwarders on the internal DNS server. Once fixed, resolution times drop and user complaints stop.

Best Practices

1. Running tests at different times of day—peak usage often reveals hidden problems.

2. Always compare results to known-good baselines—
    today's "slow" might be tomorrow's "normal."

3. Automate synthetic transactions (e.g., HTTP tests,
    pings, login scripts) using tools like PRTG, Nagios, or
    SolarWinds.

4. Correlate your findings with logs, SNMP traps, and
    user reports for a full picture.

Exam Tip #34

Expect scenario questions asking how to confirm **slow performance, high latency, or dropped connections**. Understand

1. When to use iPerf versus ping

2. What a traceroute can reveal about path congestion

3. How packet loss, jitter, and DNS delays can mimic or
    mask deeper issues

Interpreting Network Symptoms and Logs

Troubleshooting isn't just about reacting to what users say—it's about reading between the lines and using system data to confirm what's really happening. Logs are your second set of eyes: they capture what happened, when, and often why.

Whether you're looking at a core switch log or a VPN failure, interpreting logs accurately allows you to diagnose faster, eliminate guesswork, and respond confidently—especially in critical environments.

These are some of the most common log sources:

Check logs and alerts: Review logs from switches, firewalls, access points, or syslog servers.

After remediation, review logs and confirm alerts are cleared; verifying dependent services like DNS, Active Directory, or DHCP are unaffected and validate with multiple users before closing a ticket.

Router and Switch Logs

1. Record interface status changes, error counters, and routing events.

2. Useful entries include "interface down," "input errors," and "CRC mismatch."

3. Can help detect cabling issues, speed mismatches, or port failures.

Firewall Logs

1. Track allowed and denied connections by IP, port, and protocol.

2. Reveal misconfigured rules, intrusion attempts, or unexpected outbound traffic.

3. A sudden spike in denied packets may point to malware or a misapplied rule set.

Server and Authentication Logs

1. Show login attempts, service startups, shutdowns, and failed authentications.

2. Key for identifying credential issues, LDAP failures, or server-side problems impacting access.

Syslog and SIEM Platforms

1. Centralize logs from routers, switches, firewalls, servers, and more.

2. Support search filters by keyword, time, severity, or source.

3. Useful for correlation across systems, automated alerting, and audit reporting.

Key Indicators in Logs

1. **Repeated Authentication Failures**
    Often linked to brute-force attempts or misconfigured clients. Match failure times with user reports to isolate the cause.

2. **Link Flapping**
    A port going up/down repeatedly may suggest a failing cable, intermittent power loss, or hardware instability.

3. **Routing Changes or Flaps**
    BGP/OSPF instability can break routes or create latency. Frequent updates to neighbor relationships need investigation.

4. **Firewall Denials or Overly Broad Accepts**
    Denied traffic might block legitimate services. Conversely, excessive "allow" entries could suggest open paths for exfiltration.

5. **System Resource Warnings**
   Logs showing high CPU or memory usage could be tied to DDoS attacks, runaway processes, or poor device configuration.

Interpreting Symptoms in Context

Logs become most useful when paired with live user symptoms. Context is everything.

1. **Intermittent connectivity**
   Could be port flapping, wireless interference, or DHCP lease expiration.

2. **Slow applications**
   Often caused by DNS latency, retransmissions, or overloaded application servers—not always the network.

3. **Selective inaccessibility**
   If one server can't be reached, look at ACLs, route tables, or DNS resolution for that domain.

4. **Widespread disconnection**
   This points to core issues like a switch stack failure, broadcast storm, or spanning tree recalculation.

Real-World Example

A remote user reports intermittent VPN failures. On inspection, firewall logs show blocked UDP port 500—critical for IKE (VPN negotiation). The block started the same day and a new firewall policy was pushed. Rolling back the rule and testing with the user's timestamp confirms successful VPN negotiation.

Best Practices

1. **Correlate everything**: User complaints + timestamps + system logs = faster root cause analysis.

2. **Automate alerts** using your SIEM or logging platform to detect spikes or failure patterns.

3. **Retain logs per policy**: Compliance matters, and older logs are vital in root cause analysis.

4. **Don't just react—review regularly**: Routine log analysis can uncover early signs of misconfigurations, outdated software, or attempts to breach security.

Exam Tip #35

Be prepared to **analyze log entries and relate them to user-reported symptoms.**

1. A series of "interface down" messages may explain widespread disconnection.

2. Multiple failed logins with different usernames may indicate a brute-force attempt.

3. VPN failure logs tied to firewall denies help you isolate the root cause faster.

CompTIA may present you with simulated log data—read carefully and look for patterns.

Chapter Summary

In this chapter, you gained a structured and practical approach to network troubleshooting—one that balances technical analysis with methodical problem-solving. We started by breaking down the **six-step CompTIA troubleshooting methodology**, emphasizing the importance of following each stage: identifying the problem, developing and testing a theory, implementing the fix, verifying success, and documenting the outcome. This repeatable model prevents guesswork and improves consistency in high-stakes environments.

You explored **common network issues across multiple OSI layers**, from physical cable failures and duplex mismatches to misconfigured gateways and DNS errors. Knowing how to associate symptoms with their respective layers allows you to quickly isolate the root of a problem, instead of wasting time on unrelated causes. We covered the full range of **troubleshooting tools**, including physical tools like cable testers and tone generators, and software-based utilities like ping, traceroute, netstat, nmap, and Wireshark. Each tool has a specific use case, and we focused on how to use them effectively—not just what they are.

The chapter then shifted to **performance and connectivity testing**, where you learned how to diagnose slow networks using metrics like latency, jitter, packet loss, and throughput. Tools like iPerf, real-time dashboards, and DNS testing help reveal bottlenecks and ensure service-level expectations are met. Finally, we addressed how to **interpret network logs and correlate them with real-world symptoms**. Logs from routers, firewalls, switches, and authentication systems provide valuable insights—if you know what to look for. We stressed the importance of reviewing logs proactively, using timestamps and patterns to uncover root causes.

With these skills, you're not just responding to tickets—you're actively resolving problems with insight and precision. This is how you bring value as a technician: by understanding what's happening beneath the surface and taking informed action to restore service quickly and cleanly.

CHAPTER 7

Wireless Networking

Wireless networking allows devices to communicate without the use of physical cables, offering flexibility, mobility, and rapid deployment options. With the growing number of mobile devices, IoT applications, and remote work requirements, understanding wireless standards, technologies, and security measures is crucial.

In this chapter, we'll explore key wireless concepts, including radio frequency fundamentals, wireless standards (such as 802.11), configuration settings, and security protocols. You'll also learn how to optimize performance, secure wireless environments, and troubleshoot common issues.

By the end of this chapter, you will understand how to plan, implement, and manage secure wireless networks in a variety of environments.

Radio Frequency (RF) Fundamentals

Wireless networking is built on the physics of radio frequency (RF) transmission. Every decision—from access point placement to channel selection—hinges on how RF signals behave as they travel through an environment. A solid grasp of RF fundamentals helps you optimize coverage, avoid interference, and troubleshoot signal issues more effectively.

© Kodi A. Cochran 2026
K. A. Cochran, *CompTIA Network+ (N10-009) Certification Companion,*
Certification Study Companion Series, https://doi.org/10.1007/979-8-8688-2341-1_7

Frequency and Wavelength

- **Frequency** is the number of wave cycles completed per second, measured in Hertz (Hz). Higher frequencies oscillate more rapidly.

- **Wavelength** is the physical distance between wave peaks. It's inversely related to frequency—higher frequencies have shorter wavelengths.

- Shorter wavelengths carry more data but don't travel as far or penetrate obstacles as well. This trade-off shapes how and where different wireless bands are used.

Common Wireless Frequency Bands

2.4 GHz Band

- Offers better wall penetration and longer range

- **Limited capacity**: Only 3 non-overlapping channels (1, 6, and 11 in North America)

- Prone to interference from household and office devices: microwaves, cordless phones, baby monitors, Bluetooth devices

5 GHz Band

- Provides higher throughput with significantly more available non-overlapping channels

- Reduced range and wall penetration compared to 2.4 GHz

- Supports newer high-performance standards like 802.11ac and 802.11ax

- Less prone to interference due to cleaner spectrum

6 GHz Band (Wi-Fi 6E)

1. Newly available band for Wi-Fi 6E and beyond.

2. Offers a larger number of wide channels (up to 1200 MHz of additional spectrum).

   - In practical terms, 6 GHz gives you far more non-overlapping channels than 2.4 GHz or 5 GHz, which makes planning and channel reuse much easier in dense deployments.

3. Extremely low interference due to lack of legacy devices.

4. Ideal for high-density, high-throughput, latency-sensitive environments.

RF Signal Behavior

RF signals don't move through space in a straight, unaffected line. They're constantly shaped by the materials and conditions of the environment.

1. **Attenuation**: Signal strength decreases over distance and when passing through obstacles (e.g., walls, doors, windows). Denser materials cause more attenuation.

1. **Real-world note**: Attenuation is not just theory. As a rough rule, an interior drywall wall can cost about 3–6 dB, while brick or concrete can easily cost 10–15 dB or more. Metal shelving, elevator shafts, and dense utility areas can be even worse.

2. **Reflection**: Smooth surfaces like glass or metal bounce RF signals back, causing duplicate paths (multipath interference) that may cancel or distort signals.

   1. **Real-world note**: Reflections of glass and metal often create multipath, where multiple copies of the signal arrive slightly out of sync. That can look like "ghost" signals and cause rapid SNR swings, especially as users move.

3. **Refraction**: When RF waves pass through materials of differing densities (e.g., glass to air), they bend. This shift can distort coverage patterns.

4. **Diffraction**: RF waves bend around obstacles like corners or furniture. It can be helpful for coverage but weakens the signal.

5. **Scattering**: Irregular surfaces or small objects (e.g., foliage, cluttered workspaces) break up signals into multiple paths, reducing signal clarity.

6. **Absorption**: Materials like brick, concrete, and water (including human bodies) absorb RF energy. This is one of the primary causes of signal loss indoors.

Understanding these behaviors helps you make sense of dead zones, signal bounce, or performance degradation in certain parts of a building.

Signal-to-Noise Ratio (SNR)

1. **SNR** is the ratio between the strength of the wireless signal and the background noise level.

2. A **high SNR** (e.g., 30 dB or more) indicates a clean signal with strong performance potential.

3. A **low SNR** leads to retries, dropped packets, and reduced throughput—even if signal strength appears strong.

4. Noise can come from neighboring Wi-Fi networks, poorly shielded electronics, or even fluorescent lighting.

Always measuring both **signal strength** and **noise floor**—tools like Wi-Fi analyzers and spectrum analyzers can help quantify these metrics.

SNR quick guide (typical):

1. **< 10 dB**: Unusable/unstable connection

2. **10 dB**: Poor (drops, retries, low throughput)

3. **20 dB**: Fair (usable, but performance is inconsistent)

4. **30 dB**: Good (stable for most workloads)

5. **40+ dB**: Excellent (high performance potential)

Channel Overlap and Interference

Wireless channels are slices of spectrum used for communication. When multiple networks use overlapping or the same channels, interference occurs.

1. **Co-Channel Interference (CCI)**: Happens when multiple APs operate on the same channel. Devices share airtime and compete for transmission.

2. **Adjacent Channel Interference (ACI)**: Caused when APs use channels that partially overlap (e.g., 2, 3, 4 in the 2.4 GHz range). This interference is more disruptive than CCI.

3. In the **2.4 GHz band**, only channels **1, 6, and 11** are truly non-overlapping in North America.

4. In the **5 GHz and 6 GHz bands**, there are more non-overlapping channels, allowing better separation and performance.

Proper channel planning is critical, especially in high-density environments. Overlapping channels often explain unexplained drops in performance.

Best Practices

1. Conduct a wireless site survey before deploying access points—don't guess.

2. Use only non-overlapping channels (1, 6, 11 for 2.4 GHz).

3. Minimize adjacent APs using the same or adjacent channels.

4. Position APs to avoid signal contention zones— avoid placing multiple APs in the same room unless signal levels are carefully managed.

5. Use directional antennas or power tuning where appropriate to contain signal spread.

When troubleshooting in 2.4 GHz, watch for hidden nodes and wideband noise sources (e.g., poorly shielded devices or microwave leakage) that can cause retries even when RSSI looks fine. Plan channel reused intentionally. Co-channel interference is shared contention on the same channel, while adjacent-channel interference is overlap that creates corruption—adjacent interference is usually worse.

Real-World Example

An office reports constant video call disruptions. The entire wireless network is operating on 2.4 GHz, with access points set to overlapping channels (3, 4, 5). A site survey confirms significant adjacent channel interference. Reconfiguring the APs to channels 1, 6, and 11 resolves the problem almost immediately.

Exam Tip #36

Expect exam questions about RF signal behavior, channel selection, and interference patterns. Be able to

1. Identify how attenuation, reflection, or diffraction affect signal propagation

2. Determine which channels to use in 2.4 GHz environments

3. Recognize the difference between co-channel and adjacent channel interference

802.11 Wireless Standards and Technologies

Wireless networking is built on the **IEEE 802.11 family of standards**, which define how wireless devices communicate at Layer 1 (physical) and Layer 2 (data link). Over time, these standards have evolved to support higher throughput, greater efficiency, and better spectrum usage. As a network professional, your role is to understand what each version offers, how it behaves in real-world environments, and how to design networks around both new and legacy devices.

Knowing the differences between 802.11 standards allows you to

1. Match network design to user and application needs

2. Troubleshoot connectivity or performance discrepancies

3. Support mixed environments with multiple device generations

Overview of Major 802.11 Standards

Standard	Frequency band	Max speed	Channel width	Notable features
802.11a	5 GHz	54 Mbps	20 MHz	Shorter range, less interference
802.11b	2.4 GHz	11 Mbps	22 MHz	Long range, heavy interference, legacy devices
802.11g	2.4 GHz	54 Mbps	20 MHz	Backward compatible with 802.11b

(continued)

Standard	Frequency band	Max speed	Channel width	Notable features
802.11n	2.4/5 GHz	600 Mbps	20/40 MHz	Introduced MIMO, dual-band
802.11ac	5 GHz	1.3 Gbps+	20–160 MHz	MU-MIMO, wider channels, higher efficiency
802.11ax	2.4/5/6 GHz	9.6 Gbps+	20–160 MHz	OFDMA, BSS Coloring, Wi-Fi 6/6E

Note   Maximum speed is theoretical and depends on environmental factors, channel width, and client capabilities.

Key Wireless Technologies and Enhancements

These technologies are not limited to one standard—many of them build on each other to improve performance and scalability.

MIMO (Multiple Input, Multiple Output)

1. Uses multiple antennas to send and receive multiple data streams simultaneously

2. Increases throughput and reliability, especially in environments with multipath interference

3. Introduced in 802.11n

MU-MIMO (Multi-User MIMO)

1. Allows an AP to communicate with multiple clients at the same time (downlink)

2. Reduces airtime competition and boosts performance in high-density deployments

3. Introduced in 802.11ac; expanded in 802.11ax to support uplink MU-MIMO

OFDMA (Orthogonal Frequency Division Multiple Access)

1. Splits channels into subchannels (resource units), allowing parallel communications with multiple clients

2. Greatly reduces latency and improves efficiency in environments with many small data transfers (e.g., IoT, VoIP)

3. Exclusive to 802.11ax (Wi-Fi 6)

BSS Coloring

1. Allows overlapping APs on the same channel to identify each other and manage contention more effectively

2. Reduces co-channel interference without needing additional channels

3. Introduced in Wi-Fi 6

Beamforming

1. Directs the RF signal toward a specific client instead of broadcasting equally in all directions

2. Improves signal strength, range, and client stability

3. Standardized in 802.11ac (previously proprietary in 802.11n)

With explicit beamforming (802.11ac and 802.11ax), the client provides feedback so the AP can steer energy accurately. Earlier implicit approaches were often vendor-specific and "guessed" without that feedback, so results varied.

Channel Bonding

1. Combines two or more adjacent channels to increase total bandwidth

2. 802.11n allowed 40 MHz; 802.11ac and 802.11ax support up to 160 MHz

3. Higher throughput but more susceptible to interference

Backward Compatibility Considerations

1. **802.11n** supports both 2.4 and 5 GHz and remains compatible with 802.11a/b/g clients.

2. **802.11ac** is 5 GHz-only but supports 802.11n clients on that band.

3. **802.11ax (Wi-Fi 6)** supports both 2.4 and 5 GHz, and **Wi-Fi 6E** extends into the 6 GHz band. It remains compatible with earlier clients but will limit features like OFDMA and MU-MIMO when talking to older devices.

Compatibility is a major design concern in mixed environments. Legacy clients can slow down entire APs due to airtime fairness issues—use band steering and modern client policies where possible.

Real-World Example

A university upgrades its access points to 802.11ax (Wi-Fi 6) across campus. Student-owned laptops and phones vary widely—some support Wi-Fi 6, others only 802.11n. The Wi-Fi 6-capable devices immediately benefit from reduced latency and higher throughput due to MU-MIMO and OFDMA, especially in dorms and classrooms. However, the older devices continue connecting via legacy protocols and experience slower speeds when competing for airtime.

To balance performance, IT enables **band steering** and **client load balancing**, pushing newer devices to 5 GHz while reserving 2.4 GHz for older clients. Performance stabilizes across all client types.

Best Practices

1. **Avoid overprovisioning 2.4 GHz Aps**: It adds interference with little benefit.

2. **Prioritize 5 GHz and 6 GHz** for performance-critical environments.

3. **Use modern standards** (802.11ac/ax) for dense client populations.

4. **Design for backward compatibility** but limit legacy support where possible—phase out 802.11b/g clients.

5. **Enable performance features** like MU-MIMO and OFDMA only where clients can use them.

Exam Tip #37

Expect CompTIA to ask about

1. Which **802.11 standard** to deploy in specific environments

2. How **MU-MIMO**, **OFDMA**, or **beamforming** improve performance

3. Differences between **Wi-Fi 5 (802.11ac)** and **Wi-Fi 6 (802.11ax)**

4. Backward compatibility and legacy device limitations

Wireless Access Point (AP) Configuration

A wireless access point (AP) is more than just a radio transmitter—it's a strategic control point for signal coverage, device access, and traffic flow. Proper AP configuration plays a direct role in wireless performance, reliability, and security. Misconfigured APs can result in interference, dropped connections, or even open the network to exploitation. This section outlines core and advanced AP settings you'll need to understand for real-world deployments and for the Network+ exam.

Basic AP Configuration Settings

SSID (Service Set Identifier)

1. The network name that devices see when scanning for available wireless connections.

2. It should be **unique and descriptive** (e.g., Staff-Wi-Fi, Guest-Network), especially in environments with multiple SSIDs.

   - **Best practice**: Keep SSIDs short (32 characters max) and avoid sensitive terms like "Admin" or "Corp" that advertise internal intent.

3. Avoid default names like Linksys or NETGEAR—these invite confusion and make your network a more obvious target for spoofing.

SSID Broadcast

1. By default, APs broadcast their SSIDs so clients can discover them.

2. Hiding an SSID does **not provide security**—determined attackers can still see hidden networks using simple sniffing tools.

   - Hidden SSIDs still respond to probe requests and are easy to spot in a capture. Tools like Wireshark or Kismet will still show the network, so hidden does not equal secure.

3. Hidden SSIDs can complicate client configuration and roaming.

Frequency Band Selection

1. Modern APs often support both **2.4 GHz and 5 GHz** simultaneously (dual-band).

2. 2.4 GHz provides longer range and wall penetration but suffers from interference.

3. 5 GHz offers higher speeds and more channels, ideal for high-density environments.

4. Let the AP auto-select where possible but override manually when coverage is needed.

Channel Assignment

1. Set APs to use **non-overlapping channels** to reduce interference.

    -   For 2.4 GHz, only channels 1, 6, and 11 are non-overlapping in North America.

2. In crowded environments, **manual channel tuning** is often more effective than auto-selection.

3. Use a site survey tool to avoid co-channel and adjacent-channel interference.

Channel Width

1. Wider channels (e.g., 40 or 80 MHz) support higher throughput.

2. In dense environments, narrower channels (20 MHz) may reduce interference and improve performance overall.

3. Use 80 or 160 MHz **only if the spectrum is clean** and client density allows.

Transmit Power

1. Adjust transmit power to match the space:

    - **Too high**: Causes overlapping coverage, roaming issues, and interference

    - **Too low**: Causes dead zones and weak signal areas

2. Lowering power can help limit bleed-through into adjacent areas or buildings.

Advanced Configuration [Options]

AP Mode (Root, Repeater, Mesh)

1. **Root mode**: The AP serves client devices and is connected via Ethernet to the network.

2. **Repeater mode**: Extends range by relaying traffic from another AP—may reduce performance—and in many designs, it effectively halves available throughput while adding latency.

3. **Mesh mode**: Forms a self-healing wireless mesh with other APs, useful where cabling is impractical Keep in mind that each wireless hop adds overhead, so throughput and latency are usually worse than a wired backhaul.

Band Steering

1. Encourages dual-band devices to connect to the **5 GHz band**, where more bandwidth is available.

2. Helps offload congested 2.4 GHz channels automatically.

Load Balancing

1. Distributes client connections across nearby APs to prevent a single AP from being overloaded

2. Useful in dense public spaces like stadiums or auditoriums

Client Isolation

1. Prevents wireless clients on the same SSID from communicating directly with one another.

2. **Essential for guest networks** to enhance privacy and mitigate lateral attacks.

VLAN Support

1. Allows you to assign different SSIDs to separate VLANs

   - For example, Staff → VLAN 10, Guests → VLAN 20, IoT → VLAN 30

2. Enables segmentation and policy enforcement at the network layer

In controller-managed wireless networks, this SSID-to-VLAN mapping is what lets you centralize segmentation and apply consistent policies across many APs.

Real-World Example

A hotel installs multiple access points to provide Wi-Fi to guests across several floors. To protect privacy, the network admin enables **client isolation** and assigns guest traffic to a **dedicated VLAN**, preventing devices from seeing each other and keeping them segmented from the hotel's internal systems. After deployment, a site survey confirms strong signal levels without channel overlapping or interference.

Best Practices

1. Always use **WPA3** encryption when available; fall back to WPA2 only if absolutely necessary.

2. Keep firmware up-to-date to patch vulnerabilities and improve performance.

3. Use **band steering**, **client load balancing**, and **auto-channel features**—but validate them with real-world testing.

4. Standardize SSID naming conventions across locations to simplify management.

Exam Tip #38

Expect scenario-based questions involving AP configurations. You may be asked

1. Why client devices fail to connect despite seeing the SSID.

2. How to improve performance in a congested 2.4 GHz deployment.

3. What happens when transmit power is too high or when channels are misconfigured.

4. How VLAN tagging per SSID contributes to security.

Wireless Security Standards and Encryption Protocols

Securing wireless networks isn't optional—it's foundational. Every packet transmitted through the air is vulnerable to interception. That's why encryption, authentication, and proper protocol selection are critical for every wireless deployment—from home Wi-Fi to enterprise mesh networks.

Wireless security has evolved significantly since the early days of WEP. As threats have grown more sophisticated, standards have been forced to adapt. Today's best practices favor strong, dynamic encryption, centralized authentication, and a layered security approach.

Wireless Security Standards

Each generation of wireless security protocol was designed to address the weaknesses of its predecessor. Understanding the timeline and limitations of each is key to both exam questions and real-world auditing.

WEP (Wired Equivalent Privacy)

1. The original 802.11 encryption protocol—now considered completely broken

2. Used **RC4 stream cipher** with static encryption keys

3. Vulnerable to attacks using widely available tools (e.g., aircrack-ring), and can be cracked in seconds.

4. **Should never be used** under any circumstance.

WPA (Wi-Fi Protected Access)

1. Released as a stopgap while WPA2 was being developed.

2. Introduced **TKIP (Temporal Key Integrity Protocol)** to dynamically generate keys.

3. Improved over WEP but still **insecure by today's standards**—susceptible to key reinstallation and replay attacks.

4. No longer recommended in any production environment.

WPA2

1. Introduced **AES-CCMP** (Advanced Encryption Standard with Counter Mode and CBC-MAC Protocol) for strong encryption

2. Became the standard for over a decade—still widely in use

3. More secure than WPA but not immune to issues:

- Vulnerable to brute-force attacks if weak PSKs are used

- Susceptible to KRACK (Key Reinstallation Attack) if devices are not patched

WPA3

1. The current standard for wireless security

2. Uses **SAE (Simultaneous Authentication of Equals)** instead of PSK

3. Provides **forward secrecy**, meaning session keys cannot be derived even if credentials are compromised later

4. Stronger resistance to **offline brute-force** and **dictionary attacks**

5. Includes protections for public/open networks using **OWE (Opportunistic Wireless Encryption)**

Authentication Methods

Authentication methods define how users and devices are validated before being granted access to a wireless network. In simple terms, they control *who* can connect and *how* that identity is verified. Wireless authentication can be as open as allowing anyone to connect with no credentials, or as strict as requiring each device to present a unique certificate and authenticate through a centralized server.

The chosen method impacts both security and user experience—weak methods like shared passwords are easy to manage but pose serious risks, while enterprise-grade methods provide strong security with more administrative overhead. Understanding the differences between these approaches is essential for designing secure and scalable wireless environments.

Open (No Authentication)

1.   No password, no encryption.

2.   Suitable only for captive portals or guest networks with **absolutely no sensitive data**.

3.   Traffic can be intercepted and modified—**never use in environments with compliance requirements**.

Pre-Shared Key (PSK)

1.   Shared password entered on all devices

2.   Easy to configure but risky:

   - A leaked key compromises every device using it.

   - Hard to rotate without disrupting users.

   - Some environments use dynamic PSKs (unique per user or device) to keep the simple PSK workflow while eliminating shared-credential risk and simplifying revocation.

3.   Still common in small businesses and home networks.

Enterprise Mode (802.1X)

1. Uses centralized authentication with **RADIUS servers** tied to an identity source (e.g., Active Directory, LDAP)

2. Supports per-user credentials, dynamic key generation, and auditability

3. Enables certificate-based or username/password logins via **EAP (Extensible Authentication Protocol)**

4. The gold standard for **enterprise security**

This model underpins WPA2-Enterprise and WPA3-Enterprise deployments, where each user session gets unique keys and you gain stronger audit trails than a shared passphrase.

Encryption Protocols

Encryption protocols determine how wireless data is protected while in transit over the air. When devices communicate on a wireless network, they broadcast data that can potentially be intercepted—encryption ensures that intercepted data cannot be understood or tampered with.

These protocols define the algorithms and processes used to scramble data, verify its integrity, and secure communication sessions. Some, like TKIP, were once considered secure but are now outdated and vulnerable. Others, like AES-CCMP and SAE, provide strong, modern protection suitable for today's threat landscape. Choosing the right encryption protocol is critical for maintaining confidentiality, preventing tampering, and complying with security standards.

TKIP

1. Legacy encryption introduced with WPA

2. Adds message integrity checks and per-packet keying—but is now considered obsolete

3. Fails to meet modern cryptographic standards and **should be disabled** wherever possible

TKIP is considered weak today because it relies on legacy RC4-era design and has practical attack history. It is generally not acceptable for environments that must meet strong encryption expectations (e.g., payment or health-related networks).

AES-CCMP

1. The backbone of WPA2 and WPA3 encryption

2. Offers **strong confidentiality and integrity** using AES with CBC-MAC

3. Required for all modern secure Wi-Fi deployments

SAE (Simultaneous Authentication of Equals)

1. Replaces PSK in WPA3 (SAE is based on the Dragonfly key exchange)

2. Performs a **zero-knowledge key exchange**, ensuring the password is never exposed—even if the handshake is captured

3. Resistant to dictionary attacks and offers forward secrecy

Because SAE negotiates fresh session keys, capturing one handshake does not help an attacker decrypt other sessions—and it removes many of the risks that come with one shared password.

Real-World Example

A mid-sized enterprise initially uses WPA2-PSK for all employees and guest Wi-Fi. After a security audit reveals the PSK was reused across departments—and leaked externally—the organization transitions to **WPA2-Enterprise** with **802.1X authentication** backed by Active Directory. Each user now logs in with their domain credentials, and keys are rotated per session. This not only boosts security but also improves logging and accountability.

Best Practices

1. **Use WPA3** wherever supported. It provides the strongest protection.

2. If WPA3 is unavailable, use **WPA2 with AES**—and avoid TKIP.

3. Rotate shared passwords frequently if using PSK.

4. In large environments, implement **802.1X with RADIUS** for individualized access control.

5. Disable legacy protocols like **WEP**, **WPA**, and **TKIP** in all WLAN configurations.

6. Use **certificate-based authentication** (EAP-TLS) for maximum security in enterprise deployments.

Exam Tip #39

CompTIA expects you to

1. **Differentiate between WEP, WPA, WPA2, and WPA3** in terms of encryption type and weaknesses.

2. Understand when to use **PSK vs. 802.1X**, and why shared keys can pose a risk.

3. Identify **encryption protocol types** like TKIP vs. AES and what standards they're tied to.

4. Know how WPA3 improves security over WPA2—particularly with SAE and forward secrecy.

Wireless Site Surveys and Planning

Before deploying a wireless network, you need to understand the physical and environmental conditions where it will operate. That's the purpose of a **wireless site survey**—a systematic process of evaluating signal behavior, identifying sources of interference, and determining the best locations for access points. A site survey isn't just about coverage—it's about designing a network that balances performance, security, scalability, and reliability.

Site surveys help eliminate dead zones, reduce co-channel interference, and ensure that your deployment matches the real-world needs of the users, building layout, and client density. Whether you're planning a brand-new deployment or troubleshooting an underperforming network, survey data is your foundation.

Types of Site Surveys

Passive Site Survey

1. The survey tool listens passively to Wi-Fi traffic without connecting to any network.

2. Captures

   - Detected SSIDs and BSSIDs

   - Signal strength and noise floor

   - Channel usage and interference

3. Best used to **analyze the existing RF environment**—ideal for verifying coverage or planning changes in a live network.

Active Site Survey

1. The surveying device actively **connects to the network being tested.**

2. Measures

   - Actual throughput

   - Packet loss

   - Roaming performance

3. Best for **validating quality of service (QoS)** and determining real-world user experience—essential in production environments

Predictive Site Survey

1.   Performed **before any hardware is deployed.**

2.   Uses floor plans, wall material data, antenna specs, and expected user load to simulate RF behavior

3.   Conducted in software using tools like Ekahau or AirMagnet

4.   Ideal for **new construction or early-stage planning**

Site Survey Tools

1.   **Software-based**
     Tools like **Ekahau**, **AirMagnet Survey**, and **NetSpot** allow technicians to visualize coverage, simulate RF propagation, and build heatmaps.

2.   **Hardware-based**
     Devices such as **spectrum analyzers** and **laptops with dual-band Wi-Fi adapters** collect signal strength, SNR, and interference data.

3.   **Mobile-based**
     Apps for smartphones and tablets offer basic surveying functionality. Useful for spot checks, but **less accurate** than dedicated tools.

Examples: Wi-Fi Analyzer (Android) and AirPort Utility (iOS) are useful for quick spot checks, even though dedicated tools are more accurate.

Planning Considerations

Planning doesn't end once you place the APs—it involves continuous awareness of how the environment influences wireless behavior. These are the critical factors to assess

Coverage Area

1. Ensure complete signal coverage without oversaturating.

2. Account for

   - Floor layouts

   - Wall composition

   - Ceiling height

   - Furniture and equipment

Client Density

Plan for peak usage—not just average conditions. A common planning baseline is 25–30 clients per AP, then adjust up or down depending on the workload (voice/video, streaming, or mostly light browsing). In high-density areas, features like band steering and client load balancing help distribute dual-band clients across 5 GHz radios and nearby APs instead of overloading a single access point.

Also, accounting for transient spikes—for example, foot traffic in hallways or lobby areas can briefly increase contention and absorption during peak hours. Add APs in high-density areas like conference rooms, auditoriums, or dormitories.

Interference Sources

1. Identify **non-Wi-Fi sources** of signal disruption:

   - Microwaves

   - Bluetooth devices

   - Wireless cameras

   - Elevators and motors

2. Use spectrum analyzers to detect hidden noise sources.

Channel Assignment

1. Avoid channel overlap:

   - Use **non-overlapping channels** (1, 6, 11) in 2.4 GHz.

   - In 5 GHz/6 GHz, **Dynamic Frequency Selection (DFS)** allows access to additional clean channels—but may require careful tuning.

2. Manual channel planning is often more reliable than auto-channel settings.

Antenna Selection

1. **Omnidirectional antennas** spread signal in all directions—ideal for open rooms or floor coverage.

2. **Directional antennas** concentrate signal in one direction—useful for hallways, outdoor bridges, or targeted long-range links.

Caution   High-gain antennas can extend range, but they also narrow the vertical coverage pattern. Align antennas carefully—a few degrees off can create signal nulls or dead zones above/below the intended coverage.

Documentation and Validation

1. Generate heatmaps to visualize actual coverage vs. theoretical plans—including signal strength, SNR/noise, interference, and (when available) client load.

2. Document

   - AP model and placement

   - SSID and VLAN mapping

   - Channel and power settings

3. After deployment

   - Conduct a **post-installation survey** to confirm assumptions.

   - Adjust AP placement or settings based on real-world measurements.

Real-World Example

A university is renovating an older academic building. IT conducts a **predictive site survey** using digital blueprints and planned AP locations. After installation, a **passive validation survey** reveals poor signal penetration into stairwells and restrooms due to thick concrete walls. The team repositions a few APs and swaps omnidirectional antennas for directional ones—eliminating the weak coverage zones without adding extra hardware.

Best Practices

1. Always conduct both **pre-deployment** and **post-deployment** surveys—RF environments change.

2. Re-survey regularly as office layouts, furniture, and client counts evolve.

3. Tune AP power and antenna orientation as part of ongoing optimization.

4. Document every change—good records support faster troubleshooting.

Exam Tip #40

Be able to compare **passive, active, and predictive surveys**. Expect questions like

1. Which survey type to use during planning vs. post-deployment?

2. How to detect interference using survey data?

3. How to interpret heatmaps or signal strength metrics?

CompTIA may also give you diagrams or output from survey tools and ask you to choose the best action.

Troubleshooting Wireless Connectivity Issues

Even in well-designed environments, wireless networks can suffer from instability, interference, or poor user experience. Unlike wired connections, Wi-Fi relies on radio waves that are easily influenced by walls, interference, client behavior, and even environmental changes like room layout or humidity.

Troubleshooting wireless problems requires more than checking signal strength. You need to systematically observe symptoms, validate conditions with tools, analyze logs, and understand how the RF environment interacts with client behavior. Knowing which tool to use and which layer to investigate first helps you isolate root causes efficiently. During troubleshooting, look for hidden nodes and wideband noise sources in the 2.4 GHz band.

Common Wireless Symptoms and Their Causes

Weak Signal or Dead Zones

1. Caused by

   - Excessive distance from the AP

   - Thick walls, metal structures, or dense materials

   - Low transmit power or poorly aimed antennas

2. Solutions:

   - Relocate or add access points.

   - Use directional antennas or wireless repeaters.

   - Boost transmit power carefully—don't oversaturate.

Frequent Disconnections

1. Causes include

    - Signal interference (co-channel or non-Wi-Fi)

    - APs overloaded with too many clients

    - Firmware bugs or driver instability

2. Fixes:

    - Check for channel overlap.

    - Limit max client load per AP.

    - Update AP and client firmware regularly.

Slow Speeds

1. Often the result of

    - Signal attenuation or poor SNR

    - Channel congestion or excessive retransmissions

    - Bandwidth saturation (too many clients or large downloads)

2. Troubleshoot with

    - Throughput tests (e.g., iPerf)

    - Spectrum analysis to detect interference

    - Load balancing across available APs

Authentication Failures

1. May be due to

    - Incorrect PSK or expired certificate

    - Misconfigured RADIUS server or VLAN assignment

    - SSID mismatch or misapplied security settings

2. Recommended checks:

    - Review wireless logs and authentication server responses.

    - Verify SSID settings and ensure correct security protocol is used.

Inability to Roam Between APs

1. Root causes:

    - Mismatched SSIDs or VLANs between APs

    - Lack of support for fast roaming protocols

    - Sticky clients that don't hand off until signal is unusable

2. Fixes:

    - Standardize SSID and security settings across Aps.

    - Enable 802.11r/k/v (fast roaming and assisted roaming).

    - Tunes transmit power and enable band steering to encourage proper transitions.

Tools for Wireless Troubleshooting

No single tool gives you the full picture—troubleshooting requires cross-verification between wireless tools, system logs, and user feedback.

1. **Wi-Fi Analyzer Apps**
   Visualize signal strength, channel usage, SNR, and AP overlap. Ideal for identifying coverage gaps and overlap issues.

   - **Examples**: Wi-Fi Analyzer (Android) and AirPort Utility (iOS). For Wi-Fi 6E, confirm the tool supports 6 GHz analysis.

2. **Spectrum Analyzers**
   Detect non-Wi-Fi interference like microwaves, Bluetooth, or rogue devices. Essential when interference is suspected but not visible in Wi-Fi tools.

3. **Ping/Traceroute**
   Help verify IP-level connectivity, detect dropped packets, and confirm if delays are wireless or upstream network-related.

4. **Syslogs/SNMP Data**
   Collected from APs, wireless controllers, or firewalls. Useful for spotting connection denials, high error rates, firmware faults, or radio resets.

Real-World Example

In a corporate conference room, users report Wi-Fi disconnections during meetings. Basic tests show good signal strength and no DHCP issues. A **spectrum analyzer** reveals that a wireless HDMI projector is flooding the

2.4 GHz band with interference. The IT team responds by reassigning APs in that area to **5 GHz channels** and repositioning antennas to minimize signal bleed. The connection drops stop completely.

Best Practices

1. **Standardize SSID names and security settings** across all APs to support seamless roaming.

2. Use **VLAN segmentation** to isolate traffic types (e.g., guest, staff, IoT).

3. Continuously monitoring **environmental changes**—new furniture, walls, or equipment can distort RF behavior.

4. Regularly update both **AP firmware** and **client wireless drivers** to fix bugs and improve stability.

Exam Tip #41

On the exam, expect questions that present a symptom and ask for the most likely cause or best next step.

You should know how to

1. Match tools like **Wi-Fi analyzers**, **syslogs**, or **spectrum analysis** to specific problems

2. Identify interference versus authentication issues

3. Interpret symptoms like dropped connections, slow throughput, or roaming failures in a layered troubleshooting process

Chapter Summary

In this chapter, you built a strong foundation in wireless networking—a critical area in modern IT environments. We began by examining how **radio frequency (RF) signals behave**, including how attenuation, interference, and environmental factors impact performance. You learned why channel planning, signal-to-noise ratio, and proper antenna configuration matter in every deployment.

You explored the evolution of the **IEEE 802.11 standards**, from 802.11a through Wi-Fi 6 (802.11ax) and Wi-Fi 6E, gaining an understanding of how features like **MU-MIMO**, **OFDMA**, **beamforming**, and **channel bonding** enhance throughput, reliability, and user density. Knowing which standard to use and when is essential for supporting today's applications and client devices. We covered **access point (AP) configuration** in depth, focusing on settings that influence signal coverage, bandwidth, and security posture. Topics included SSIDs, transmit power, VLAN tagging, band steering, and load balancing—all of which contribute to a stable and secure wireless experience.

You reviewed **wireless security protocols**, from legacy WEP and WPA to modern, hardened options like **WPA2 with AES** and **WPA3 with SAE**. We explained key **authentication methods**, including PSK and enterprise-level 802.1X using RADIUS and certificate-based controls, highlighting their relevance in scalable, policy-driven environments. In deployment planning, you learned how to perform and interpret **wireless site surveys**—passive, active, and predictive—using both software and hardware tools. This process ensures access points are placed strategically and performance expectations are met before users even connect.

Finally, we walked through **wireless troubleshooting strategies**, focusing on real-world symptoms like dropped connections, slow speeds, and roaming failures. You now know how to identify causes using tools such as Wi-Fi analyzers, spectrum analyzers, ping, logs, and SNMP alerts.

Together, these skills empower you to design, secure, and maintain reliable wireless networks—whether in a small business, university campus, or enterprise facility.

Wireless Quick Reference Table

Category	Feature	Details
Frequency bands	2.4 GHz	Longer range, higher interference, 3 non-overlapping channels
	5 GHz	Shorter range, more bandwidth, cleaner spectrum
	6 GHz (Wi-Fi 6E)	High throughput, minimal interference, ideal for dense use
Common standards	802.11n	Dual-band, MIMO, up to 600 Mbps
	802.11ac	5 GHz, MU-MIMO, wider channels, up to 1.3 Gbps+
	802.11ax (Wi-Fi 6)	2.4/5/6 GHz, OFDMA, BSS coloring, up to 9.6 Gbps+
Wireless security	WPA2	AES encryption, widely used
	WPA3	SAE authentication, forward secrecy, modern standard
Encryption protocols	TKIP	Legacy, insecure, used in WPA

(continued)

Category	Feature	Details
	AES-CCMP	Strong encryption used in WPA2 and WPA3
Authentication modes	PSK	Shared key, easier setup, less secure
	802.1X	Enterprise-grade, RADIUS-based, dynamic credentials
Survey types	Passive	Listens only, collects SSIDs and signal data
	Active	Connects to test throughput and roaming
	Predictive	Simulates coverage using blueprints and software
Troubleshooting tools	Wi-Fi Analyzer	Shows signal strength, channel overlap, SSID presence
	Spectrum Analyzer	Detects non-Wi-Fi interference like Bluetooth or HDMI

CHAPTER 8

Network Hardening and Security Practices

Securing a network isn't just about perimeter defenses or access policies—it starts at the device level. Network hardening is the process of reducing the attack surface of individual components like routers, switches, firewalls, servers, and endpoints. Each device represents a potential entry point for attackers, especially if it's running unnecessary services or is left in a default configuration. (i.e., minimizing exploitable services, ports, or features on a device)

Hardening is about **intentional reduction**—removing what's not needed, limiting who has access, securing communication channels, and enforcing good operational hygiene. It must be part of every deployment checklist, audit process, and security standard.

Some of the most common hardening steps are the following:

Disable Unused Services and Ports

- Shut down any default services not required for operation (e.g., Telnet, SNMPv1/v2, unencrypted HTTP, plain FTP).

K. A. Cochran, *CompTIA Network+ (N10-009) Certification Companion,*
Certification Study Companion Series, https://doi.org/10.1007/979-8-8688-2341-1_8

- Close any unnecessary **open ports**—even idle services can be exploited if left accessible.

- This minimizes exposure and reduces the number of vectors attackers can probe.

Change Default Credentials

- Replace factory-set usernames and passwords immediately after deployment.

- Use **strong, unique passwords** or **key-based authentication** for each device.

- Weak or default credentials remain one of the most exploited attack vectors in real-world breaches.

Apply Firmware and OS Updates

- Firmware contains the device's operating system and must be updated regularly to patch vulnerabilities.

- Monitor vendor announcements and CVE feeds for zero-day vulnerabilities affecting your hardware (e.g., NIST NVD, MITRE).

- Schedule maintenance windows for patching and avoid relying on outdated images for device rollouts.

Use endpoint management platforms to enforce baseline security posture (BIOS/UEFI passwords, TPM presence, and Secure Boot status) so devices meet minimum requirements before they touch sensitive networks.

Enable Secure Management Interfaces

- Replace insecure remote access protocols:

  - **Use SSH instead of Telnet** for CLI access (both Layer 7).

  - **Use HTTPS instead of HTTP for web interfaces (both Layer 7).**

- Restrict administrative access by

  - **Allow listing management IPs**

  - Binding interfaces to internal VLANs or trusted subnets

  - Disabling remote admin where not needed

Implement Role-Based Access Control (RBAC)

1. Assign users **only the permissions required** for their job function.

2. Limit access to configuration, monitoring, and debugging features to trusted roles.

3. Avoid shared admin accounts—use individual credentials for accountability.

Log and Monitor Administrative Activity

1. Enable logging for

1. Login attempts (successful and failed)

2. Configuration changes

3. Interface state changes

2. Forward logs to a centralized **Syslog server** or **SIEM** for correlation and long-term retention.

Ensure systems are time-synchronized (NTP) so event timelines are reliable. For higher-assurance environments, store logs in tamper-evident or WORM storage and protect integrity with hashing or digital signatures.

Use Strong Encryption Protocols

1. Only enable **secure versions** of network protocols:

   1. **SNMPv3** instead of SNMPv1/v2

   2. **SSH** instead of Telnet

   3. **TLS 1.2 or TLS 1.3 instead of SSL or RC4**

2. Disable outdated protocols like **SSLv2/v3**, **WEP**, and any use of **MD5** for authentication.

Real-World Example

A network admin conducting a routine security audit identifies that several distribution-layer switches still permit **HTTP and Telnet access** for remote management. These services transmit credentials in plaintext, making them vulnerable to interception. The admin disables both services, enables **HTTPS** and **SSH**, and restricts access to a dedicated **management VLAN**. All configuration changes are logged and pushed to a central repository using automation tools. This not only strengthens security but also ensures compliance with the organization's hardening standards.

Best Practices

1. Establish a **baseline configuration standard** for each device type—and enforce it.

2. Harden all devices **before deployment** into production environments.

3. Perform **regular compliance audits** using config scanning tools or scripts.

4. Use automation platforms like Ansible, Chef, Puppet, or vendor-native tools to apply and maintain hardening consistently.

Exam Tip #42

Expect Network+ exam questions that ask you to

1. Identify insecure services (e.g., Telnet, SNMPv2) and their secure replacements

2. Choose appropriate hardening steps for routers, switches, or wireless APs

3. Recognize the risks of default credentials or open ports

4. Understand why and how management interfaces should be restricted

Administrative Controls and Network Policies

Securing a network involves more than firewalls and encryption—it also requires well-defined policies and procedures that govern *how* users interact with systems. These are known as **administrative controls**: organizational policies that reduce risk, reinforce accountability, and guide secure behavior.

While technical controls (like firewalls or access control lists) enforce restrictions on software or hardware, administrative controls define **who** has access, **under what conditions**, and **how changes are managed**. These controls are essential in supporting legal compliance, standardizing operations, and reducing the risk of human error or insider threats.

Securing a network isn't just about perimeter defenses or access policies—it starts at the device level. Network hardening is the process of reducing the attack surface of individual components like routers, switches, firewalls, servers, and endpoints. Each device represents a potential entry point for attackers, especially if it's running unnecessary services or is left in a default configuration.

Using IP allows management interfaces to restrict administrative access to trusted networks. Differentiate technical controls (hardware/ software mechanisms) from administrative controls (policies/processes) and physical controls (environmental safeguards). Note enforcement mechanisms for administrative policies, such as revoking access, HR discipline, or mandatory retraining.

Acceptable Use Policy (AUP)

1. Defines how users are allowed to interact with organizational assets (e.g., computers, networks, the Internet).

2. Prohibits behaviors like installing unauthorized
    software, using work devices for personal business,
    or visiting malicious websites.

3. Helps organizations enforce discipline and justify
    action when users misuse systems. Enforcement
    can include revoking access, HR discipline, or
    mandatory retraining.

Least Privilege Principle

1. Users and processes should only have **the
    minimum access required** to perform their
    function—no more, no less.

2. Reduces

    - Risk of accidental misconfiguration

    - Potential damage from compromised accounts

    - Lateral movement in case of breach

3. Often enforced using **role-based access controls
    (RBAC)** and permissions auditing.

Change Management Policy

1. Requires all system, software, or configuration
    changes to follow a **review and approval process**

2. Minimizes unexpected downtime, config drift,
    and uncoordinated updates (config drift refers to
    unintended configuration changes over time that
    cause inconsistencies across systems).

3. Supports traceability—all changes should be logged and tested in staging before production.

Separation of Duties

1. Critical tasks are divided across multiple individuals or departments to **prevent abuse of power or insider threats**.

2. Examples:

   - The person who develops a patch should not be the one who approves or deploys it.

   - Financial systems often separate the ability to approve, submit, and audit transactions.

3. Enforced both procedurally and via permissions.

Security Awareness Training

1. Empowers users to recognize and avoid threats like phishing, social engineering, or data mishandling.

2. Should cover

   - Password best practices

   - Secure use of remote access tools

   - How to identify suspicious activities

3. Regular refresher training reduces human-related vulnerabilities—often the weakest link in security. Organizations should schedule formal awareness training annually or quarterly and reinforce it with simulated phishing campaigns and scenario-based assessments.

Network Access Controls

In addition to policies, certain **technical controls** help enforce those policies at the network edge. These are often layered with administrative requirements to control who connects to the network and under what conditions. Often used in conjunction with badge access and biometrics.

MAC Filtering

1. Allows or denies access based on device MAC address.

2. Easy to implement but **not secure**—MAC addresses can be spoofed.

3. It is still useful in temporary setups or for isolating specific devices.

Port Security

1. Configured at the switch level to

    - Limit the number of devices on a port

    - Tie ports to known MAC addresses

    - Shut down or alert on unauthorized connections

2. Helps protect against unauthorized plug-ins or rogue devices.

Network Access Control (NAC)

1. NAC systems enforce **health checks** before allowing a device to join the network.

2. Verifies

   - Antivirus status

   - OS patch levels

   - Configuration compliance

3. Devices that fail posture checks can be **quarantined** or denied access until remediated.

Real-World Example

An organization's internal policy requires all configuration changes to follow a formal **change management process**. During an audit, it's discovered that a junior admin bypassed this process to troubleshoot a device—inadvertently causing a network outage. The incident triggers a review that leads to implementing stricter **separation of duties** and requiring approval before applying any changes to production systems. The process is logged, automated through configuration management tools, and tied back to a central change ticket system for accountability.

Best Practices

1. Review and update **administrative policies annually** or after major incidents or audits.

2. Where possible, **enforce policy using technical controls** (e.g., NAC, RBAC, ACLs).

3. **Log all access requests, approvals, and configuration changes**, and store them in a centralized system.

4. Map policies to frameworks like **NIST 800-53, PCI-DSS, HIPAA**, or **ISO/IEC 27001** to support compliance efforts.

Exam Tip #43

Be ready to distinguish **administrative controls** from **technical controls**. Know how to

1. Apply policies like **least privilege, separation of duties, and acceptable use.**

2. Enforce these policies through technical safeguards like **NAC** and **port security.**

3. Recognize that **procedures and training** are just as vital as firewalls and encryption.

Physical and Environmental Security Controls

Network infrastructure is only as secure as the physical space it resides in. While technical controls guard against cyber threats, **physical and environmental controls** defend against theft, tampering, environmental damage, and unauthorized access to critical equipment.

These controls are particularly important in **data centers, IDF/MDF closets, remote branches, and co-location environments**, where even a moment of unmonitored physical access can result in device compromise or service disruption. Regular refresher training reduces human-related vulnerabilities—often the weakest link in security.

Physical security measures, also known as physical controls, are safeguards put in place to prevent unauthorized physical access to network infrastructure and sensitive hardware. These controls aim to protect assets from theft, tampering, sabotage, or environmental damage. Integrate feeds with NVRs or security dashboards for real-time monitoring.

Physical Security Measures

Physical security measures, also known as physical controls, are safeguards put in place to prevent unauthorized physical access to network infrastructure and sensitive hardware. These controls aim to protect assets from theft, tampering, sabotage, or environmental damage. Unlike technical controls (which protect digital systems through firewalls, encryption, and access control lists), and administrative controls (which govern policies and procedures), physical controls mitigate risks in the tangible environment where systems operate.

Physical security includes everything from **locked doors and badge readers** to **video surveillance, mantraps, and biometric authentication systems**. Unlike logical or technical controls that restrict digital access, physical controls operate in the **real-world space** where devices reside, ensuring that only authorized personnel can interact with or affect critical systems.

Access Control Systems

1. Enforce entry through **keycards, biometric readers, PIN pads, or staffed checkpoints.**

2. Physical access should be logged—preferably integrated into a centralized monitoring system.

3. Doors to IDF/MDF rooms or server spaces should automatically lock when closed. Access control logs should be monitored and integrated with SIEM platforms for real-time alerting and correlation with other security events.

Mantraps and Turnstiles

1. Dual-door systems that allow only one person to enter at a time.

2. Prevent **tailgating** or **piggybacking**, especially in highly secure facilities.

3. Often used in conjunction with badge access and biometrics. Mantrap systems should enforce multi-factor authentication (MFA) and time-based access rules for sensitive areas.

Locking Cabinets and Racks

1. Prevent unauthorized tampering with switches, patch panels, or servers.

2. Useful in shared spaces (e.g., co-locations) or unsecured branches.

    - For mobile endpoints in sensitive roles, consider physical asset tagging (RFID or GPS) to support inventory tracking and loss prevention.

3. Combine with tamper-evident seals for audit compliance. Use electronic lock systems that can log cabinet access and integrate with centralized identity management systems.

Surveillance Systems

1. CCTV cameras act as both deterrents and evidence collectors.

2. Coverage should include

   - Server room entrances

   - Wiring closets

   - Perimeter access points

3. Integrate feeds with NVRs or security dashboards for real-time monitoring. Ensure all surveillance data is time-stamped, encrypted at rest, and access-controlled (least privilege). In larger environments, centralize CCTV through a video management system (VMS) to enforce retention, support analytics, and simplify investigations.

Visitor Logs and Escort Policies

1. All non-authorized individuals should sign in and be escorted. Logs should capture the purpose of the visit, the assigned escort, and the areas accessed.

2. Maintain records for audits or forensic reviews, and store them in secure, auditable systems.

Environmental Controls

Environmental controls are systems and safeguards designed to **protect network and computing equipment from damage caused by environmental factors** such as heat, humidity, water, fire, and power instability. These controls maintain optimal operating conditions within data centers, server rooms, and infrastructure closets.

Common examples include **HVAC systems** for temperature and humidity regulation, **fire suppression systems**, **uninterruptible power supplies (UPS)**, **generators**, and **environmental monitoring sensors**. While often overlooked, these controls are essential for maintaining **network uptime**, **hardware longevity**, and **operational continuity**—especially in mission-critical environments.

HVAC (Heating, Ventilation, and Air Conditioning)

1. Prevents overheating, condensation, and electrostatic buildup

2. Critical for ensuring continuous operation of servers, switches, and UPS units

Where possible, place power and cooling systems on independent circuits to reduce the chance of cascading failures from a single breaker, PDU, or upstream fault. Modern facilities often use zone-based cooling and hot/cold aisle containment to move air efficiently. Pair HVAC with IoT-enabled sensors (temperature, humidity, airflow) feeding centralized dashboards so cooling alerts can be escalated before outages occur.

Fire Detection and Suppression

1. Combine **smoke detectors** with **non-liquid suppression systems:**

    - FM-200

    - CO_2 gas

    - Dry powder (in specific cases)

2. Avoid water-based sprinklers near electronics unless
   no alternative exists.

Use door interlocks and clear signage to prevent entry during clean-agent discharge tests or maintenance windows. For clean-agent systems (e.g., FM-200), verify concentration levels and retention times per vendor and facility policy.

Uninterruptible Power Supplies (UPS)

1. Provide temporary power during brief outages.

2. Allow systems to **safely shut down** or maintain
   operations until generators start.

3. Sizing should match the **critical load and
   runtime** needed.

Test UPS units quarterly under realistic load to validate runtime expectations and battery health.

Generators and Backup Power

1. Used for **prolonged outages**, especially in primary
   data centers.

2. Fuel supply, auto-start features, and **routine testing**
   are essential.

Environmental Monitoring Systems

1. Deploy sensors for

   - Heat spikes

- Humidity deviations

- Water leaks

- Air quality or dust

2. Alerts should be integrated with NOC dashboards or SNMP traps.

Real-World Example

A regional bank's data center loses utility power due to a city-wide outage. UPS **activates immediately**, keeping all network and core systems online. Within 15 seconds, the diesel generator engages. Throughout the event, **HVAC systems remain active**, preserving environmental conditions. Logs from **access control** and **surveillance systems** confirm that no unauthorized access occurred. The event is documented in the institution's incident report and reviewed for procedural improvements.

If intrusion detection is in scope for the facility, route intrusion alerts into the same centralized logging and notification workflow so the security team can respond quickly and correlate events. Connect environmental sensors (temperature, humidity, smoke, water-leak) to an alerting platform and define escalation paths to on-call staff. Water-leak detection is especially important around raised floors, drip pans, and HVAC units.

Best Practices

1. Use **layered physical controls**: Door locks, card access, cameras, and policies.

2. Inspect **fire suppression, HVAC, and power systems** regularly.

3. Integrate **environmental and physical logs with logical security systems** for end-to-end visibility.

4. Limit physical access based on job roles and operational need.

Exam Tip #44

Expect questions on how **environmental and physical controls protect uptime** and security. Know the role of

1. UPS vs. generators

2. FM-200 vs. water suppression

3. Mantraps vs. basic access control

4. How surveillance and visitor policies support auditing

Remote Access and VPN Security

Remote access is no longer optional—it's essential. Whether employees work from home, connect to cloud platforms, or travel with mobile devices, the **ability to securely access internal resources from anywhere** is a foundational part of modern IT.

VPNs (Virtual Private Networks) provide secure tunnels over untrusted networks like the Internet. But without proper configuration, **VPNs themselves can introduce vulnerabilities**. Strong authentication, endpoint compliance, and encryption are non-negotiable components of secure remote access. Audit and rotate VPN credentials or certificates periodically.

Types of Remote Access

Client VPN (Remote Access VPN)

1. Allows individual users to connect to the network via software clients

2. Encrypts traffic between the user's device and the organization's network

3. Common in **work-from-home and mobile worker** environments

Site-to-Site VPN

1. Establishes **permanent encrypted tunnels** between branch offices or partner networks.

2. Traffic between locations flows securely without user intervention.

3. Often configured on **firewalls or routers**.

Cloud-Based VPN Services

1. VPN infrastructure is hosted and maintained by **third-party providers**.

2. Offers simplified deployment and management for small or hybrid teams.

3. May include **SaaS integrations** and **global access points**.

Secure VPN Protocols

A **secure VPN protocol** is a set of rules and technologies that **encrypt and protect data transmitted over a virtual private network (VPN)**, ensuring confidentiality, integrity, and authentication between endpoints. It creates a **private tunnel through untrusted networks**, such as the Internet, to safeguard communication between users and organizational resources.

To be considered secure, a VPN protocol should

1. Use **strong encryption algorithms** (e.g., AES-256)

2. Support **secure key exchange methods** (e.g., Diffie-Hellman, IKEv2)

3. Provide **authentication mechanisms** for endpoints (e.g., digital certificates, pre-shared keys)

4. Prevent **man-in-the-middle attacks, packet sniffing, and session hijacking**

5. Be **regularly maintained and vetted** by the security community

Replace insecure protocols with more secure alternatives: avoid Telnet, SNMPv1/v2, unencrypted HTTP, and plain FTP. Ensure visitor logs capture the purpose of visit, assigned escort, areas accessed, and are stored in secure, auditable systems. Use endpoint management platforms to enforce BIOS passwords, TPM presence, and Secure Boot status. Secure evidence storage rooms with multi-factor authentication, surveillance, and audit trails; use fireproof and tamper-evident cabinets.

IPSec (Layer 3)

1. Encrypts and authenticates IP packets

2. Supports both remote and site-to-site configurations

3. Uses protocols like AH (Authentication Header) and ESP (Encapsulating Security Payload)

SSL/TLS (Layer 7)

1.   Browser-based VPN portals or clients

2.   Useful for accessing web-based applications or when network-level access is not needed

L2TP over IPSec

1.   Provides tunneling features of L2TP with the encryption of IPSec

2.   Still used in legacy systems or devices lacking native IPSec support

IKEv2

1.   Robust VPN protocol with **support for mobile reconnection**, always-on behavior, and fast negotiation

2.   Ideal for **BYOD**, **smartphones**, and **roaming users**

VPN Security Enhancements

1.   **Multi-Factor Authentication (MFA):**
     Prevents credential-only logins by requiring tokens, biometrics, or authenticator apps.

2. **Split Tunneling:**

   Allows users to access local (Internet) and corporate resources at the same time
   Use with caution—improperly configured, it can expose internal traffic.

3. **Always-On VPN:**

   Automatically initiates a secure tunnel whenever the device connects to a network.
   Great for ensuring consistent security without relying on user action.

4. **Endpoint Compliance Checks:**

   Devices are evaluated for antivirus status, patch level, or OS version before granting access.
   Helps prevent untrusted or compromised endpoints from connecting.

Real-World Example

An engineering firm uses an **IPSec VPN** for remote employees. Users log in via company-issued laptops using **MFA tokens** and pass a **compliance check** confirming current AV status and OS patching. Once authenticated, they're connected to internal engineering servers over a **fully encrypted tunnel**. VPN logs are fed to a **SIEM** platform for audit and anomaly detection.

Best Practices

1. Enforce **MFA** on all remote access.

2. Use **the most secure VPN protocols** available (IPSec or SSL/TLS).

3. Configure and monitor **split tunneling** appropriately.

4. Log all VPN access and **correlate with endpoint posture** and user behavior.

5. Audit and rotate VPN credentials or certificates periodically. Ensure VPN client software and firmware are kept updated to address vulnerabilities.

Exam Tip #45

Know the differences between

1. **Site-to-site vs. remote access VPNs**

2. **IPSec vs. SSL/TLS**

3. Best practices like MFA, split tunneling risks, and endpoint compliance Understand implications of split tunneling and when to disable it.

Expect questions asking how to configure a **secure remote access solution** or troubleshoot VPN failures.

Logging, Evidence Handling, and Forensics Readiness

Network hardening is not limited to proactive prevention; it also requires a reactive framework for when an incident occurs. To survive an audit or a legal investigation, an organization must maintain trustworthy logs and standardized forensic procedures.

For logs to be useful during an investigation, they must be accurate and untampered:

- **Time Synchronization**: Ensure all log sources are synchronized via **NTP**, ideally using redundant time sources, to ensure incident timelines are legally and technically defensible.

- **Log Integrity**: Store logs in **tamper-evident** or **WORM (Write Once, Read Many)** systems.

- **Verification**: Use digital signatures or hashing to detect alterations and validate the integrity of log data during an investigation.

- **Retention Policy**: Formally define retention periods in your security policy, specifying exactly what data is kept, for how long, and for what purpose.

Secure Backups and Removable Media

Securing data at rest is as critical as securing the live network:

- **Encryption**: Encrypt all backup data (utilizing hardware-backed encryption where available) and store the encryption keys separately from the backup sets.

- **Geographic Diversity**: Maintain at least one geographically separated backup location and conduct hardware audits during quarterly compliance reviews.

- **Removable Drive Controls**: For mobile storage, implement remote wipe and geofencing capabilities.

- **Secure Transport**: Treat the physical transport of removable media as a security event that requires formal logging and approvals.

Evidence Collection and the Chain of Custody

If a breach leads to legal action, the "Order of Volatility" and proper documentation are paramount:

- **Order of Volatility**: During incident response, prioritize capturing **volatile data** (RAM, process tables, and active connections) before shutting down a system.

- **Hashing**: Hash all evidence using **SHA-256** (and MD5 for redundancy where legally permitted). Store these hashes separately from the evidence and validate them automatically during intake.

- **Chain of Custody**: Use standardized forms (following **ISO/IEC 27037** or **SWGDE** guidance) to document the history of the evidence. Include contextual notes such as the system state and the logged-in users at the time of collection.

Forensics Operations and Storage

The environment where evidence is analyzed must be as secure as the evidence itself:

- **Access Requirements**: Personnel handling forensics must undergo background checks and sign confidentiality agreements in addition to having restricted technical access.

- **Analysis Lab**: Maintain an isolated forensic analysis lab with strictly restricted access.

- **Physical Storage**: Secure physical media in fireproof, tamper-evident cabinets protected by multi-factor authentication (MFA) and audit trails.

- **Readiness Validation**: Regularly test your forensic traceability and chain-of-custody handoffs using **red-team/blue-team exercises**.

Configuration Management and Change Control

A secure network isn't just about setting strong passwords or using encryption—it's also about **ensuring that device settings are consistent, intentional, and documented over time**. That's the role of configuration management and change control.

Configuration management ensures that routers, switches, firewalls, and endpoints are built, deployed, and maintained using a well-good standard. **Change control** governs how and when those configurations can be modified, minimizing the risk of outages, misconfigurations, or unauthorized changes.

Together, these practices reduce downtime, improve security, and support auditing and compliance across even the most complex networks.

Configuration Management

Configuration management is the practice of systematically defining, organizing, and maintaining the settings, policies, and operational parameters of devices and systems across a network. Its primary purpose is to ensure that **all devices remain consistently configured**, meet organizational security policies, and can be **quickly restored** to a known-good state if something goes wrong.

This process helps organizations

1. Maintain **standardized configurations** across routers, switches, firewalls, and endpoints

2. Detect **unauthorized or accidental changes**

3. Support **auditing, compliance**, and **incident recovery**

4. Enable automation and repeatable deployments. Configuration-as-Code (CaC) tools like Ansible, Puppet, or Terraform can automate baseline deployment and remediation.

Configuration management includes tools and practices for **baselining, version control, automated enforcement**, and **compliance validation**. It reduces the risk of misconfiguration—a leading cause of outages and security vulnerabilities—and provides clear visibility into the current state of the network.

Baseline Configurations

1. Define a well-good setup for each device role.

2. Used to

   - Detect unauthorized or accidental changes

- Restore systems after misconfiguration or compromise Supports rollback through automated tools or command-line configuration archives.

- Enforce standardization across locations. Should be version-controlled and stored securely in a configuration management database (CMDB) or Git repository.

Automated Configuration Tools

1. Platforms like **Ansible**, **Puppet**, **Chef**, and vendor-native systems (e.g., Cisco DNA, Juniper Contrail)

2. Benefits include

   - Bulk deployment

   - Rollback on failure

   - Audit logging

3. Enforce consistency across distributed environments without manual repetition. Integrate with CI/CD pipelines for continuous deployment of secure configurations. Use playbook versioning to track automation logic changes over time.

Version Control and Backup

1. Track configuration changes over time to

   - Troubleshoot regressions

   - Perform root cause analysis

   - Meeting audit requirements

2. Always maintain offline backups in case of device failure or ransomware events. Store backups securely with encryption-at-rest and periodic integrity checks. Schedule automated exports to offline or immutable storage (e.g., WORM drives or air-gapped locations).

Configuration Validation

1. Tools and scripts can

    - Compare current configs to baseline templates

    - Scan for policy violations (e.g., open ports, deprecated protocols)

2. Help maintain alignment with compliance standards (e.g., NIST, PCI, CIS Benchmarks). Automate daily or weekly config scans with alerts for non-compliant changes

Change Control Processes

Change control refers to the structured process an organization uses to **evaluate, approve, document, and implement changes to its IT environment**—including configurations, systems, applications, or infrastructure. The primary goal is to ensure that all changes are made **deliberately, safely, and with accountability**, reducing the risk of downtime, misconfiguration, or security gaps.

Effective change control

1. Requires that **all changes are planned**, not ad hoc

2. Involves a **formal request and approval workflow**

3. Ensures changes are **tested before deployment**

4. Includes a **rollback plan** in case something goes wrong

5. Results in **clear documentation** for auditing and troubleshooting

This process is essential for **minimizing unplanned outages**, maintaining security, and complying with standards like **ITIL, NIST**, or **PCI-DSS**. It also improves team coordination by making sure stakeholders are aware of upcoming changes that could affect systems or services.

Formal Change Requests

1. Required for any configuration, software, or hardware modification

2. Should include

   - Scope and purpose of change

   - Risk assessment

   - Rollback plan

   - Approval chain Assign unique Change Request IDs (CRIDs) to track and audit each change.

Scheduled Implementation Windows

1. Changes should occur during maintenance windows to limit business impact.

2. Notifications should be sent to stakeholders, help desks, and affected users in advance. Ensure configuration snapshots or backups are taken immediately before execution. Define blackout periods where changes are restricted (e.g., end-of-quarter, peak business hours).

Testing and Rollback Procedures

1. Ideally, test changes in **staging or lab environments** before production rollout.

2. Rollback steps must be documented and ready to implement in case of failure. Leverage configuration version control tools (e.g., Git, RANCID) for instant reversion.

Post-Change Documentation and Validation

1. Verify that the change produced the expected outcome (e.g., ACL applied, traffic rerouted).

2. Update

    - Network diagrams.

    - Configuration repositories.

    - Inventory and versioning systems Record pre- and post-change performance metrics (e.g., latency, throughput) to confirm operational impact. Attach logs and validation artifacts (e.g., command outputs, screenshots) to the CR record for audit.

Real-World Example

An engineer is tasked with updating firewall policies at 30 branch locations. Instead of logging in manually to each site, they use an Ansible playbook to push the new configuration. The system checks syntax and interface availability before applying changes. If any device becomes unreachable during the update, Ansible **automatically rolls back to the previous version**. All actions are logged in the configuration management database (CMDB) and presented in the weekly change control meeting— demonstrating both technical precision and policy compliance.

Best Practices

1. **Integrate configuration management and change control** together.

2. Use **role separation**: One person submits the change, another approves, a third implements.

3. Maintain centralized, **version-controlled config repositories.**

4. **Audit regularly** to identify configuration drift and policy gaps.

5. Automate wherever possible—human error is still one of the biggest sources of network failure.

Exam Tip #46

Be prepared to

1. Recognize the value of **baselines, automation,** and **version control**.

2. Understand how change control processes minimize risk.

3. Identify proper change request components (e.g., scope, rollback, approval).

4. Know how tools like **Ansible or Puppet** help enforce consistent configurations.

Network Hardening Quick Reference Table

Category	Control/feature	Description
Device hardening	Disable unused services	Reduce attack surface (e.g., disable Telnet, HTTP)
	Strong passwords/ change defaults	Prevent unauthorized access
	Secure protocols	Use SSH, HTTPS, SNMPv3 instead of legacy alternatives
Administrative controls	AUP, least privilege, separation	Reduce insider threats and enforce accountability
	Security awareness training	Educate users on phishing, social engineering, hygiene
Physical security	Access control, mantraps, cameras	Prevent unauthorized physical access
Environmental controls	HVAC, UPS, fire suppression	Maintain safe operating conditions and ensure uptime
Remote access	VPN + MFA	Secure external connections with encryption and authentication
	Always-on VPN, split tunneling	Automate secure access; control Internet-bound traffic
Configuration management	Version control, automation	Maintain consistent, validated settings
Change control	Requests, approvals, rollbacks	Safely implement, track, and document modifications

Network Hardening Checklist

This can be used as a standard checklist for field technicians and auditors to ensure that devices and infrastructure are secured to the best practices. Use automation platforms like Ansible, Chef, or vendor-native tools to apply and maintain hardening consistently.

Device Configuration and Security

1. Disable unused services (e.g., Telnet, HTTP, SNMPv1/v2).

2. Change default admin credentials on all devices.

3. Enforce strong password policies or implement key-based access.

4. Enable secure protocols (SSH, HTTPS, SNMPv3, TLS 1.2+).

5. Apply latest firmware and OS patches.

6. Restrict management access by IP or VLAN.

7. Limit login attempts to prevent brute-force attacks.

8. Enable logging of admin access and configuration changes.

9. Configure role-based access control (RBAC).

10. Back up device configurations regularly. Enable control plane policing (CoPP) to rate-limit potentially malicious traffic to routers and switches. Disable unused physical interfaces or set them to shutdown state. Apply MAC address filtering or port security on switch access ports.

Administrative Controls

1. Acceptable Use Policy (AUP) is defined and enforced.

2. Least privilege access model implemented.

3. Change management policy in place and followed.

4. Security awareness training conducted regularly.

5. Separation of duties enforced for critical roles. Conduct regular user access reviews to identify dormant or excessive privilege accounts. Implement multi-person control for sensitive configuration tasks (e.g., dual approval or quorum-based changes).

Physical Security Controls

1. Server rooms and IDF/MDF closets are physically locked.

2. Access controlled via keycards, PINs, or biometrics.

3. Mantraps or turnstiles in use (where appropriate).

4. Racks and cabinets are locked and labeled.

5. CCTV cameras monitor all sensitive physical areas.

6. Visitor logs maintained; escorts required for guests. Ensure equipment is above floodplain level (raised floor or elevated racks where applicable). Set up automated alerts from environmental sensors via SNMP or syslog integration.

Environmental Safeguards

1. HVAC system maintains proper temperature and humidity.

2. Fire suppression system installed (FM-200, CO_2 preferred).

3. UPS installed for critical systems.

4. Backup generator tested regularly.

5. Environmental monitoring system tracks temperature, water leaks, etc.

Remote Access and VPN

1. VPN access requires multi-factor authentication (MFA).

2. Strong protocols in use (e.g., IPSec, IKEv2, TLS).

3. Split tunneling reviewed and restricted as needed.

4. Endpoint compliance checks required before connection.

5. Always-on VPN deployed for mobile devices (if applicable).

6. VPN logs integrated into centralized SIEM. Disable VPN access for unused or terminated accounts automatically through IAM sync. Restrict VPN usage by time-of-day or geographic location, if policy allows.

Configuration and Change Management

1. Baseline configurations defined for all device types.

2. Automated tools (e.g., Ansible, Puppet) used for deployments.

3. Configuration changes logged and version-controlled.

4. Formal change approval process in place.

5. Rollback procedures documented and tested.

6. Post-change validation and documentation performed periodic drift detection scans against baselines to ensure config integrity. Automate ticket creation for detected unauthorized config changes.

Monitoring and Logging

1. Centralized logging in place (e.g., SIEM, syslog aggregation).

2. Admin activity and authentication events logged.

3. Network health and performance monitored (SNMP, NetFlow, etc.).

4. Alerts configured for unauthorized access or device changes.

5. Regular log reviews conducted for anomalies. Use DNS logging to detect suspicious domain resolutions. Use machine learning-based anomaly detection where available (e.g., UEBA in SIEM).

Chapter Summary

In this chapter, you explored the core strategies and practical measures used to **harden network infrastructure** and safeguard it against internal and external threats. We began with **device hardening**, focusing on how to reduce the attack surface by disabling unnecessary services, changing default credentials, applying firmware updates, and enforcing secure management protocols like SSH and HTTPS. You then examined **administrative controls** that support secure operations, including acceptable use policies (AUP), least privilege enforcement, separation of duties, and structured change management. These controls help ensure that technical configurations are supported by clear policies and human accountability.

The chapter also detailed **physical and environmental security controls**, reinforcing that uptime and data protection depend on more than just logical defenses. Access control systems, surveillance, locking cabinets, HVAC, fire suppression, UPS systems, and generators were highlighted as essential layers of physical resilience. With the rise of remote work, we explored **VPN security**, comparing client-based and site-to-site solutions. You reviewed protocols such as IPSec, IKEv2, and SSL/TLS, along with advanced practices like multi-factor authentication, endpoint compliance checks, split tunneling management, and always-on VPN configurations.

Finally, we covered **configuration management and change control**—two disciplines that enforce consistency, reduce misconfigurations, and ensure network changes are deliberate, documented, and reversible. Tools like Ansible and Puppet, along with proper testing, rollback, and versioning practices, were emphasized for their role in secure operations and compliance. Collectively, these techniques form the backbone of a hardened, secure, and resilient network infrastructure—capable of supporting confidentiality, integrity, and availability in today's complex and distributed environments.

CHAPTER 9

Network Monitoring and Performance

Whether you're responsible for a small branch office or a globally distributed enterprise, your ability to see what's happening on the network determines how quickly you can respond to problems. **Network monitoring** is more than a single dashboard—it's an ecosystem of protocols, tools, and practices that help you maintain uptime, enforce service-level agreements, and detect anomalies before they become outages. In this chapter, we'll build on the foundations laid in earlier chapters by examining the protocols and platforms used to collect data, the metrics that describe performance, and the logging systems that turn raw events into actionable insight.

By the time you've finished this chapter, you should feel confident in choosing the right tool for the job, defining meaningful thresholds, and interpreting trends. As with other topics in this book, a blend of practical examples, best-practice checklists, and exam tips will prepare you for both real-world troubleshooting and certification questions.

For the exam, be prepared to match protocols to their purpose. SNMP collects operational metrics; Syslog forwards event messages; NetFlow/ sFlow/IPFIX captures flow metadata; and ICMP supports reachability tests like ping and traceroute. Questions may also quiz you about the secure versions (e.g., SNMPv3) and default ports (e.g., SNMP uses UDP 161/162).

© Kodi A. Cochran 2026
K. A. Cochran, *CompTIA Network+ (N10-009) Certification Companion*,
Certification Study Companion Series, https://doi.org/10.1007/979-8-8688-2341-1_9

Core Monitoring Protocols

Monitoring begins with the protocols that devices use to export information. Each protocol operates at a different OSI layer and is designed for a specific type of data. Understanding their strengths and limitations will help you build a more comprehensive monitoring solution.

- **SNMP (Simple Network Management Protocol)**: A standards-based protocol primarily working at the application layer. SNMP agents expose counters such as CPU utilization, interface status, and temperature to a manager. While legacy versions (v1 and v2c) are unencrypted and rely on community strings, SNMPv3 adds authentication and encryption—choose it whenever the platform supports it. SNMP typically uses UDP 161 for queries and UDP 162 for traps/ information.

  - SNMP traps are asynchronous messages triggered by events such as interfaces going down or CPU spikes, allowing devices to notify managers without being polled.

- **Syslog**: A logging protocol rather than a metric exporter. Routers, switches, firewalls, and servers forward their event messages to a central collector (or SIEM). Syslog defines severity levels (e.g., emergency, alert, critical, warning, informational) and categories so you can filter and act on what matters most. Syslog typically uses UDP 514 (some environments use TCP 514), and secure deployments may use Syslog over TCP/TLS.

- Syslog message formats can vary. BSD-style Syslog (RFC 3164) is common, while structured Syslog (RFC 5424) is more consistent for parsing and correlation.

- **NetFlow/sFlow/IPFIX**: Flow-based protocols capture metadata about conversations on your network: who is talking to whom, which protocols are in use, and the volume of data transferred. NetFlow (Cisco) and IPFIX (IETF) are similar; sFlow samples packets at Layer 2 or 3 and is common on switches. A common NetFlow export port is UDP 2055, and exporters should throttle or sample as needed so collectors aren't overwhelmed during spikes.

- **ICMP (Internet Control Message Protocol)**: Best known for its diagnostic utilities like ping and traceroute. ICMP echoes can tell you if a device is reachable, how long packets take to travel between hops, and whether intermediate routers are dropping or delaying traffic. ICMP type 8 is Echo Request and type 0 is Echo Reply.

Some routers and firewalls rate-limit or block ICMP to reduce DDoS amplification and reconnaissance. Treat ping and traceroute results as one data point, not absolute proof of reachability.

Best Practices

Before we examine tools, keep these protocol-level practices in mind:

- **Prefer secure versions**: Use SNMPv3 rather than v1/v2c; use encrypted channels when forwarding Syslog messages; restrict flow exports to trusted collectors. When confidentiality and integrity matter, consider Syslog over TCP/TLS (often referred to as RFC 5425) instead of sending logs over UDP in clear text.

- **Limit scope**: Only enable the protocols you actually need on devices and limit who can poll or collect data by using access lists.

- **Align polling intervals with impact**: Critical interfaces may require sub-minute polling; less important devices can be polled every few minutes to reduce overhead.

Real-World Example

At a large university, network engineers configured **SNMPv3** on all core routers and switches. A monitoring platform polls CPU and interface counters every 30 seconds. When an access switch reports a 50 °C temperature spike, the monitoring tool sends an immediate alert. Technicians discover a cooling fan has failed and replaced it before users notice any slowdown. Without encrypted SNMP and rapid polling, the failure might have gone undetected until the switch shut down entirely.

Exam Tip #47

For the exam, be prepared to match protocols to their purpose. *SNMP* collects operational metrics; *Syslog* forwards event messages; *NetFlow/ sFlow/IPFIX* captures flow metadata; and *ICMP* supports reachability tests like ping and traceroute. Questions may also quiz you about the secure versions (e.g., SNMPv3) and default ports (e.g., SNMP uses UDP 161/162).

Network Monitoring Tools

Once protocols are enabled, you need tools to display and act on the data. Tools range from lightweight command-line utilities to enterprise platforms that integrate alerts, graphs, and configuration management. Choose a combination that fits your environment and budget.

- **Ping/Traceroute**: The humble ping sends ICMP echo requests to verify reachability and measure round-trip time. Traceroute expands on this by revealing each hop between a source and a destination, helping you isolate where latency or packet loss occurs.

- **Wireshark**: A graphical packet analyzer that captures and decodes frames in real time. It's invaluable when diagnosing mysterious performance issues, security incidents or protocol misbehavior. Because it can see payloads, use it judiciously and ethically.

- **Nmap**: A scanning tool that discovers hosts and services on a network. By probing ports, it identifies which services are listening to and, in many cases, what software versions are running. Administrators often use Nmap to audit for unexpected open ports or to verify firewall rules.

- **Nagios/Zabbix/PRTG**: Popular open-source and commercial monitoring suites. They poll devices via SNMP, collect flow data, and render dashboards showing CPU, memory, interface utilization, and latency. You can define alerts, create custom scripts and integrate them with ticketing systems.

- **SolarWinds/ManageEngine**: Enterprise platforms that scale thousands of devices. In addition to performance monitoring, they offer configuration management, network mapping, and reporting.

- **SIEM Platforms (e.g., Splunk, QRadar, LogRhythm)**: Although more security-focused, SIEMs ingest logs from network devices, correlate events and detect threats. Many also support performance metrics or can integrate with your monitoring tools.

Real-World Example

An enterprise uses **Ping** to monitor basic reachability and **Nmap** to ensure only approved services are exposed. When an intern accidentally enables FTP on a test server, nightly Nmap scans detect the open port. The security team is notified, shuts down the service and updates the standard build procedure to prevent a repeat. Later, Wireshark helps debug intermittent VoIP call quality issues by revealing high jitter and identifying a misconfigured QoS policy.

Best Practices

- Use **layered monitoring**: Combine high-level availability checks (ping) with deep visibility (flow and packet analysis) to catch issues that one tool alone might miss.

- **Tune alerts** to avoid fatigue: If every minor event triggers an email or SMS, people will ignore real emergencies. Group related events and set appropriate thresholds.

- **Secure access** to your monitoring systems: These platforms often have privileged credentials; enforce multi-factor authentication and keep them on a management network.

Exam Tip #48

Expect the exam to test your knowledge of what each tool does and where it fits. For example, Wireshark is used for deep packet inspection; Nmap performs port and service discovery; and Nagios monitors performance metrics and alerts when thresholds are exceeded.

Network Performance Metrics and Baselines

Having tools in place is only half the battle. To know whether a network is healthy, you need to measure it against something. **Key performance metrics** quantify latency, loss, and utilization; a **baseline** records what "normal" looks like so you can spot deviations.

Key Network Performance Metrics

- **Latency**: The time, usually in milliseconds, that it takes for a packet to travel from source to destination and back. High latency might indicate congestion, long physical distances, or inefficient routing.

- **Jitter**: The variation in latency between successive packets. Real-time applications like VoIP and video streaming are sensitive to jitter because they expect packets at consistent intervals.

- **MOS (mean opinion score)**: Is commonly used in VoIP environments to rate perceived call quality on a 1–5 scale.

- **Packet loss**: The percentage of packets that never reach their destination. Loss can be caused by congestion, faulty cables, interference in wireless links, or overloaded devices. Even small amounts of loss can degrade voice and video quality.

- **Bandwidth vs. Throughput: Bandwidth** is the theoretical maximum capacity of a link, whereas **throughput** is the actual rate at which data is successfully transferred. If throughput is significantly lower than bandwidth, look for congestion, duplex mismatches, or misconfigured quality-of-service policies.

- **Error rates**: Interface counters such as CRC errors and input drops signal physical layer problems—bad cabling, dirty fiber connectors or mismatched speed/duplex settings.

- **Availability/Uptime**: The percentage of time that a device or service is reachable. High availability isn't just a number—it depends on redundant links, hardware failover, and proper change management.

Establishing Baselines

Baselines give context to raw metrics. Without them, you won't know if 5 ms of jitter is problematic or perfectly normal for your environment.

- **Measure during typical periods**: Capture data during peak and off-peak hours so you understand the full range of normal behavior.

- **Document assumptions**: Note the business cycles, application mix, and recent changes that might affect performance. A baseline taken during a holiday break won't represent normal traffic.

- **Update after changes**: Hardware upgrades, new applications, or topology changes can alter performance; take a new baseline after each significant event.

Real-World Example

After deploying a cloud-based CRM system, a company notices that voice calls sound choppy during the mid-day rush. Baseline data collected before the deployment shows jitter of 1–2 ms. Current monitoring shows jitter spiking to 15 ms and packet loss at 2%. Flow analysis reveals that automated backups are saturating the WAN link at noon. By rescheduling backups to overnight hours and adjusting QoS settings, latency and jitter return to normal, and call quality improves.

Best Practices

- **Collect long-term data** so you can distinguish transient spikes from systemic problems.

- **Visualize metrics**: Graphs and heatmaps make it easier to spot trends and anomalies than raw numbers alone.

- **Set thresholds based on history**: Alert when metrics exceed your baseline by a defined percentage or over a sustained period, rather than on single spikes.

Exam Tip #49

The exam may ask you to differentiate between latency, jitter, and packet loss, or to interpret graphs showing throughput versus bandwidth. You should also understand the role of baselines and how they influence alert thresholds.

Logging and Alerting Systems

If metrics tell you how the network is performing, **logs** tell you what happened. Every device generates messages about configuration changes, access attempts, and errors. Collecting these logs centrally and building an effective alerting workflow turn raw events into actionable intelligence.

Syslog: A logging protocol rather than a metric exporter. Routers, switches, firewalls, and servers forward their event messages to a central collector (or SIEM). Syslog defines severity levels (e.g., emergency, alert, critical, warning, informational) and categories so you can filter and act on what matters most. Alerting channels include email, SMS, push notifications, dashboards, and integrations with ticketing or chat systems. Ensure there is clear ownership of each alert type so nothing falls through the cracks.

Logging Fundamentals

- **Log sources:** Routers, switches, firewalls, servers, operating systems, and applications all produce logs. Each provides a piece of the puzzle—for example, a firewall log might show blocked connections while an application log reveals a misconfiguration.

- **Log types:**

  - *Event logs* contain general system messages such as interface up/down notifications, and service restarts.

  - *Audit logs* record who made changes, what commands were run, and when. They are essential for compliance and forensic analysis.

- *Security logs* document intrusion attempts, blocked connections, and failed authentication. They help identify malicious activity.

- **Log management tools**: In addition to **Syslog**, consider dedicated collectors like Graylog or Logstash that can parse and normalize messages. **SIEM platforms** such as Splunk, QRadar, or LogRhythm centralize logs, correlate events across sources, and provide dashboards and reports.

Alerting Strategies

Not every log entry warrants immediate action. Effective alerting focuses attention on meaningful events and reduces noise.

- **Threshold alerts** trigger when a metric or counter exceeds a defined value (e.g., CPU > 90%, memory > 80%).

- **Anomaly alerts** use heuristics or machine learning to detect behavior that deviates from the baseline, such as a sudden surge in login attempts or outbound traffic.

  - Dynamic thresholds can adapt to time-of-day or day-of-week traffic patterns, reducing false positives during predictable busy periods. In practice, combining threshold-based and anomaly-based alerting helps catch both known conditions and emerging patterns.

- **Severity levels** help to prioritize response:

  - *Critical* events require immediate intervention (e.g., loss of a core link).

- *Warning* events indicate a developing issue (e.g., interface utilization creeping upward).

- *Informational* events are recorded for context but don't demand immediate action.

Alerting channels include email, SMS, push notifications, dashboards, and integrations with ticketing or chat systems. Ensure there is clear ownership of each alert type so nothing falls through the cracks. Many organizations integrate alerts with on-call and incident response platforms such as PagerDuty or Opsgenie for escalation and tracking. Document ownership and urgency for each alert type (e.g., "Network Team: Critical VPN alerts") so the right group is notified quickly.

Real-World Example

During a quiet weekend, a SIEM platform ingests firewall logs showing hundreds of failed SSH login attempts from the same foreign IP address. Based on correlation rules and geolocation data, the SIEM labels the activity as a **brute-force attack** and sends a critical alert to the on-call engineer via SMS. The engineer blocks the offending IP and reviews the access control lists to ensure that SSH is only allowed from trusted subnets. Later analysis of audit logs confirms there were no successful logins during the attack.

Best Practices

- **Synchronize time** across all devices (e.g., via NTP) so logs from different sources can be correlated accurately.

- **Retain logs** for as long as compliance and troubleshooting need to dictate. Storage costs are modest compared to the value of having historical data when investigating incidents.

- **Suppress noise** by filtering known harmless events and consolidating repetitive alerts. Too many alerts can be as bad as no alerts at all.

- **Test alerting workflows**: Periodically trigger test alerts to ensure the right people receive notifications and that the response processes work as expected.

Exam Tip #50

Expect questions that ask you to classify log types or choose the best alerting method for a given scenario. Make sure you understand the differences between event, audit, and security logs, and the meaning of critical versus warning alerts.

Monitoring Quick Reference Table

Tool/protocol	Primary purpose	OSI layer/category
SNMP (v1–v3)	Collect device metrics such as CPU, memory, and interface status	Application Layer
Syslog	Forward system and application logs	Application Layer
ICMP (ping/traceroute)	Test reachability and path latency	Network Layer

(continued)

Tool/protocol	Primary purpose	OSI layer/ category
NetFlow/ sFlow/IPFIX	Analyze traffic flows and bandwidth usage	Network/transport layer
Wireshark	Capture and inspect packets for deep analysis	Data link/network layer
Nmap	Discover hosts and open services	Network/transport layer
SIEM (Splunk, etc.)	Correlate logs and detect anomalies	Security analytics
SolarWinds/ Nagios	Centralized monitoring with dashboards and alerts	Multi-layer monitoring

Chapter Summary

In this chapter, you learned how monitoring protocols, tools, and practices come together to keep networks running smoothly. We began with **SNMP**, **Syslog**, **NetFlow/sFlow/IPFIX** and **ICMP**, noting which OSI layers they operate at and why secure versions matter. Then we compared common tools from simple ping and traceroute to full-featured platforms like **Nagios**, **SolarWinds**, and **SIEMs**.

Next, we explored performance metrics such as latency, jitter, packet loss, bandwidth, throughput, error rates, and availability. You saw why baselines are essential for context and how to establish them through regular measurement and documentation. A real-world example illustrated how mis-timed backups can degrade VoIP, and how flow analysis and QoS adjustments resolve the issue.

We then turned to logging and alerting. By categorizing logs into event, audit, and security types, and by using collectors and SIEMs, you can centralize data for correlation and analysis. We discussed alerting strategies—from threshold-based triggers to anomaly detection—and emphasized the importance of severity levels and testing workflows.

Finally, a **quick reference table** summarized the major protocols and tools along with their purposes and OSI layers. With these fundamentals in hand, you are prepared to design a monitoring solution that delivers visibility, supports proactive troubleshooting, and stands up to exam scenarios.

CHAPTER 10

Cloud Computing and Virtualization

If the last decade has taught IT professionals anything, it's that hardware is no longer the limiting factor it once was. A single rack of servers can host hundreds of workloads, and you can spin up an entire application stack in the cloud with a few clicks. **Virtualization** and **cloud computing** are the technologies that make this possible. They abstract physical resources into flexible, software-defined pools that you can allocate on demand, scale up or down at will, and manage through a web interface instead of a screwdriver. In this chapter, we'll demystify both concepts, explore how they complement each other and show you how to deploy them securely and efficiently.

By the end of this chapter, you'll understand why virtualization is the foundation of cloud, how hypervisors create and manage virtual machines, and what distinguishes Infrastructure, Platform, and Software-as-a-service. We'll cover different cloud deployment models, dive into the nuts and bolts of cloud networking, and address the critical security and compliance considerations that come with entrusting your data to someone else's infrastructure. Throughout the chapter we'll sprinkle in real-world stories and best practices so you can apply these concepts to your own environment.

© Kodi A. Cochran 2026
K. A. Cochran, *CompTIA Network+ (N10-009) Certification Companion,*
Certification Study Companion Series, https://doi.org/10.1007/979-8-8688-2341-1_10

Virtualization Fundamentals

At its core, **virtualization** is about making one thing look like many. Instead of dedicating an entire server to a single application and watching most of its CPU cycles go to waste, you can carve that server into multiple **virtual machines (VMs)** that each think they own their own hardware. A piece of software called a **hypervisor** sits between the physical hardware and the VMs, brokering access to CPU time, memory pages, disk blocks, and network frames. From the perspective of the operating system running inside the VM, nothing has changed—it still sees /dev/sda and eth0—but under the hood, it's sharing resources with its neighbors.

Virtualization isn't just about servers either. You can virtualize storage (creating logical disks from a pool of physical drives), networks (segmenting traffic with virtual switches and overlay networks) and even desktops (delivering entire workstation environments from a data center). Wherever there's expensive hardware that sits idle most of the time, virtualization can help you do more with less.

Why Virtualize? Key Benefits

Virtualization offers a long list of advantages over running applications directly on physical hardware. Some of the most important include

1. **Resource efficiency and consolidation**: You can run dozens of modest workloads on a single high-end server rather than spreading them across multiple low-utilization machines. This reduces capital expenses (fewer servers to buy), operational expenses (less power and cooling) and frees up rack space for future growth.

2. **Scalability and elasticity**: Need a new web server for a test project? Just clone a template VM. Expecting a surge in traffic? Spin up more instances until the storm passes and then retire them when demand drops. Hypervisors and orchestration tools make this process fast and repeatable.

3. **Isolation and security**: Each VM is encapsulated in its own sandbox. A misbehaving application or a malware infection inside one VM doesn't necessarily spread to others. You can also apply different firewall rules, VLANs, and policies to each VM.

4. **Hardware independence and portability**: Because a VM thinks it owns its hardware, you can move it from one physical host to another with minimal disruption. Technologies like **live migration** (VMware vMotion, Hyper-V Live Migration, KVM Live Migration) move a running VM across hosts without downtime. This makes maintenance less disruptive and enables load balancing across your cluster.

5. **Rapid provisioning and life cycle management**: Creating a new server is as simple as cloning a template, applying configuration scripts and powering on. Snapshots let you capture a VM's state before making risky changes; if something breaks, you can roll back in minutes. Templates ensure consistency across environments and reduce configuration drift.

6. **Test, dev, and training environments**:
   Virtualization allows you to build isolated labs on
   demand. Developers can test software on multiple
   OS versions without owning physical hardware.
   Trainers can reset student VMs with a single
   command.

7. **Disaster recovery**: Replicating a VM to a remote
   site is easier than rebuilding a bare-metal server.
   Combined with snapshotting and incremental
   backups, virtualization reduces recovery time
   objectives (RTOs) and helps meet business
   continuity goals. Define replication policies for
   critical systems (your RPO/RTO targets) and run
   disaster recovery drills so you're not learning your
   recovery process during the outage.

Hypervisor Types and Technologies

The **hypervisor** is the engine of virtualization. It abstracts physical
resources and presents them to VMs, enforcing isolation and fairness.
There are two primary categories of hypervisors:

1. **Type 1 (bare-metal) hypervisors** run directly on
   the hardware without a host operating system.
   They're purpose-built for performance and security.
   Examples include **VMware ESXi**, **Microsoft
   Hyper-V**, **KVM** (used by many Linux distributions),
   and **Xen**. Type 1 hypervisors typically support
   advanced features like high availability, distributed
   resource scheduling, live migration, and fault
   tolerance.

2. **Type 2 (hosted) hypervisors** run on top of a conventional operating system like Windows, macOS, or Linux. They're easier to install and more accessible for labs and test environments. **VMware Workstation, Oracle VirtualBox,** and **Parallels Desktop** are common examples. Because the host OS consumes resources and introduces extra layers, Type 2 hypervisors generally don't match the performance or scalability of Type 1 solutions. However, they are invaluable for developers, trainers, and hobbyists.

   - In enterprise environments, you'll commonly run into KVM on Linux, VMware ESXi/vSphere, and Microsoft Hyper-V.

Hypervisor Technologies

Beyond this basic classification, hypervisors support a host of technologies designed to improve performance and manageability:

1. **Paravirtualized drivers** (also known as virtio) expose virtual hardware interfaces that are optimized for virtualization rather than emulating physical devices. Using paravirtualized network and storage drivers reduces overhead and improves throughput.

2. **Resource schedulers** allocate CPU time, memory and I/O bandwidth among VMs. Features like VMware's Distributed Resource Scheduler (DRS) and Hyper-V's Dynamic Memory ensure that workloads get the resources they need while preventing any single VM from starving its neighbors.

3. **High availability (HA)** automatically restarts VMs on other hosts if a physical server fails. Combined with redundant storage, this minimizes downtime for critical services.

4. **Distributed virtual switches** extend the concept of a physical switch into the hypervisor cluster. They allow consistent network policies, VLAN configurations, and security rules across multiple hosts. VMware's vSphere Distributed Switch and Microsoft's Hyper-V Virtual Switch Manager are examples.

5. **Storage virtualization** technologies like VMware vSAN, Microsoft Storage Spaces Direct and Ceph aggregate local disks into a shared storage pool. This eliminates the need for dedicated SAN hardware and provides features like thin provisioning, deduplication and replication.

6. **Containerization** deserves a brief mention. While not a hypervisor-based technology, containers like Docker and Kubernetes package applications and their dependencies in isolated user spaces. Containers share the host OS kernel, making them lighter and faster to start than VMs. Many modern environments run containers inside VMs to combine the security of virtualization with the efficiency of containers.

Real-World Example

Imagine an accounting firm running half a dozen outdated physical servers: one for email, another for file sharing, three for databases, and one for a custom application. Each server's CPU hovers below 15% but power and cooling bills keep climbing. By migrating the workloads into VMs on two new virtualization hosts, the firm reduces its server count, improves fault tolerance and frees up a rack for expansion. When maintenance time arrives, the IT team uses **live migration** to move running VMs between hosts without any perceived outage to end users. This flexibility would be impossible with stand-alone physical servers.

Best Practices for Virtualization

1. **Use Type 1 hypervisors in production**: Their direct access to hardware yields better performance and security than hosted solutions. As a starting point, keep vCPU overcommit conservative (e.g., 4:1) and adjust based on workload behavior and performance metrics.

2. **Monitor host and guest resources**: Over-provisioning VMs can saturate CPU, memory, or storage and degrade performance across the cluster. Track utilization and adjust allocations as workloads change.

3. **Secure management interfaces**: Isolate hypervisor consoles and APIs onto a management network and enforce multi-factor authentication. Don't expose the hypervisor to the open Internet.

4. **Plan for resource contention and failover**: Reserve capacity so that VMs can be restarted on another host if one server fails.

5. **Keep hypervisor software up-to-date**: Vendors regularly patch vulnerabilities that could lead to VM escape or privilege escalation. Tools like Terraform (provisioning) and Ansible (configuration) help you standardize builds, reduce manual mistakes, and make environments repeatable.

6. **Document and automate**: Use templates, scripts, and Infrastructure-as-Code tools to deploy VMs consistently. Maintain an inventory of VMs, their purpose, and their owners.

Exam Tip #51

Expect the exam to ask you about the difference between Type 1 and Type 2 hypervisors, the purpose of live migration and the benefits of snapshots. You should also know why paravirtualized drivers improve performance and how HA and DRS contribute to fault tolerance and resource balancing.

Cloud Service Models: IaaS, PaaS, SaaS, and Beyond

Virtualization set the stage for cloud computing by decoupling workloads from hardware. **Cloud services** build on that foundation to deliver IT resources over the Internet on a subscription basis. Instead of buying servers, you rent compute, storage, and application capacity from a provider and pay only for what you use. Understanding the different service models will help you choose the right level of control and abstraction for each workload.

Infrastructure As a Service (IaaS)

IaaS offers virtualized compute, storage, and networking resources on demand. You manage the operating systems, applications, and data, while the provider maintains the physical hardware, virtualization layer, and facilities. This model is closest to traditional hosting but with far greater scalability and flexibility.

1. **Examples**: Amazon EC2, Microsoft Azure Virtual Machines, Google Compute Engine, Oracle Cloud Infrastructure.

2. **Use cases**: Hosting custom applications; running dev/test environments; disaster recovery sites; temporary compute farms for batch processing; self-managed container clusters.

3. **Advantages**: You have full control over the OS and runtime; you can install any software and customize network settings. Scaling infrastructure is as simple as increasing instance sizes or adding more VMs.

4. **Considerations**: You're responsible for patching the OS, securing remote access and managing backups. Without automation, IaaS environments can become sprawling and difficult to govern.

Platform As a Service (PaaS)

PaaS abstracts away from the operating system and middleware so developers can focus on writing code. The provider handles the OS, runtime, web server and language frameworks. You simply push your application and data. PaaS environments often include built-in scaling, load balancing and integration with developer tools.

1. **Examples**: Google App Engine, Microsoft Azure App Services, Heroku, Red Hat OpenShift, AWS Elastic Beanstalk.

2. **Use cases**: Rapid development of web and mobile applications; microservices architectures; serverless functions (a variant often called **FaaS— Functions as a Service**); continuous integration and continuous deployment (CI/CD) pipelines.

3. **Advantages**: Developers can deploy apps without provisioning VMs or configuring web servers. Autoscaling and patch management are handled by the provider. PaaS encourages good development practices, such as decoupling applications into microservices and storing configuration externally.

4. **Consideration**: You have less control over the underlying environment. Long-running tasks or non-standard libraries may not be supported. There's also risk of vendor locking if you adopt proprietary services tightly integrated with a single provider.

Software As a Service (SaaS)

SaaS delivers complete applications accessible via a web browser or thin client. Everything—servers, storage, code, and data—is managed by the provider. Users simply log in and use the service. This is the most abstract model and is ideal when you need productivity tools but don't want to manage any infrastructure.

1. **Examples**: Microsoft 365 (Office 365), Google Workspace, Salesforce, ServiceNow, Slack, Zoom.

2. **Use cases**: Email and collaboration suites; customer relationship management (CRM); enterprise resource planning (ERP); help desks; e-commerce platforms; project management tools.

3. **Advantages**: There's nothing to install or maintain locally. Upgrades and security patches happen automatically. SaaS offerings often integrate with other cloud services via APIs.

4. **Consideration**: Data residency and compliance can be tricky if your information remains within specific geographic borders. Customization is limited to what the provider exposes through settings and API endpoints. Subscription costs can accumulate as you add users and features.

Beyond the Basics: FaaS and CaaS

In addition to the classic trio of IaaS, PaaS, and SaaS, cloud providers offer more granular services:

1. **Functions as a Service (FaaS)**, also known as serverless computing, lets you run small bits of code in response to events without provisioning servers. AWS Lambda, Azure Functions, and Google Cloud Functions are examples. You pay only for the time your code executes.

2. **Containers as a Service (CaaS)** provides managed container orchestration platforms such as AWS Fargate, Azure Container Apps, and Google Cloud Run. It abstracts the underlying cluster while letting you package and deploy containers consistently.

Best Practices for Cloud Service Models

1. **Match the model to the workload**: Mission-critical systems that require fine-grained control may belong on IaaS, whereas commodity applications like email and CRM are well suited for SaaS.

2. **Automate provisioning**: Use Infrastructure-as-Code tools such as Terraform or CloudFormation to deploy IaaS and PaaS resources consistently.

3. **Monitor usage and costs**: Cloud billing can spiral out of control if you leave unused VMs running or scale services beyond what you need. Set budgets, configure alerts, and regularly right-size resources.

4. **Plan for portability**: Where possible, build applications on open standards and containers so you can migrate between providers.

5. **Understand the shared responsibility model**: Even in SaaS, you are responsible for data classification and access controls. In IaaS and PaaS, you manage more of the security stack.

Exam Tip #52

Be prepared to identify which service model a scenario describes and who is responsible for what. For example, in IaaS, you patch the operating system, but the provider maintains the hardware. In PaaS, you manage your code, while the provider manages the runtime and middleware. In SaaS, the provider handles everything; your job is to configure user access and data policies.

Cloud Deployment Models: Public, Private, Hybrid, and Community

While service models describe what you consume, **deployment models** describe where your cloud runs and who has access to it. Choosing the right deployment model involves balancing cost, control, security, and compliance.

Public Cloud

In a **public cloud**, resources are owned and operated by a cloud provider and shared among multiple customers (tenants). Each customer's workloads are isolated in their own virtual environment, but all share the same physical infrastructure. Public cloud offers economies of scale and is the most elastic option.

1. **Examples**: Amazon Web Services (AWS), Microsoft Azure, Google Cloud Platform (GCP), Alibaba Cloud

2. **Use cases**: Hosting web applications, development sandboxes, burst capacity during seasonal peaks, non-sensitive data storage

3. **Pros**: No capital expenditure, rapid provisioning, global presence, managed services like databases and content delivery networks

4. **Cons**: Less control over hardware and network topology, multi-tenancy introduces security considerations, data residency may be limited by the provider's regions

Private cloud

Dedicates resources to a single organization. It can be built on premises using technologies like VMware vCloud Director, OpenStack or Nutanix, or hosted by a provider on isolated hardware. Private clouds offer greater customization and governance at the cost of higher complexity and capital requirements.

1. **Examples**: VMware vCloud Foundation, OpenStack, IBM Cloud Private

2. **Use cases**: Industries with strict regulatory requirements (finance, healthcare, government); organizations that need to integrate closely with legacy systems; applications with predictable, steady workloads

3. **Pros**: Full control over security, compliance and networking; ability to tailor hardware; isolation from other tenants; easier integration with on-premises systems

4. **Cons**: Higher cost and responsibility for maintaining the infrastructure; limited scalability compared with public cloud; longer procurement cycles

Hybrid Cloud

Hybrid cloud combines public and private environments with orchestration and management that allows workloads to move between them. It's common for organizations to keep sensitive data and legacy applications on-premises while using public clouds for web front-ends or burst capacity.

1. **Examples**: VMware Cloud on AWS, Azure Arc, AWS Outposts, Google Anthos

2. **Use cases**: Disaster recovery (replicating VMs to the cloud); temporary scaling during busy periods; gradual migration of applications to the cloud; data analytics using cloud resources against on-premises data sets

3. **Pros**: Flexibility to run workloads where it makes sense; ability to satisfy compliance while still leveraging cloud innovation; smoother migration path

4. **Cons**: Increased complexity in networking and security; the need for consistent identity and access management across environments; potential for higher cost if workloads shuttle frequently

Community

Community cloud refers to infrastructure shared by organizations with similar requirements—for example, a group of hospitals sharing a HIPAA-compliant cloud managed by a third party. It balances the cost savings of a shared environment with tailored security and governance.

Multi cloud is a newer term describing the use of multiple public cloud providers simultaneously. An organization might deploy its front-end on AWS, its analytics on GCP, and its backup storage on Azure. Reasons include avoiding vendor locking, taking advantage of provider-specific features, and optimizing cost.

Real-World Example: A Hybrid Healthcare Provider

A regional healthcare network stores electronic health records in a private cloud hosted in its own data center. To deliver a telehealth application with high availability, it deploys the front-end and video streaming services in a public cloud region close to patients. Non-sensitive analytics data is processed in a third provider's serverless environment. This hybrid and multi-cloud strategy lets the organization meet regulatory requirements, minimize latency, and avoid being tied to a single vendor.

Best Practices for Deployment Models

1. **Perform a risk and compliance assessment**: Understand what data you are storing, who needs access, and what regulations apply. This will guide whether data can live in public cloud or must stay on private infrastructure.

2. **Design for portability**: Use containers, open APIs, and automation tools to reduce friction when moving workloads between environments.

3. **Unify identity and access management**: Implement single sign-on and federated identity so users have consistent credentials across clouds and on-premises. That same consistency should apply to monitoring and logging, so alerts and incident response work the same way across platforms.

4. **Ensure consistent networking and security policies**: Tools like software-defined WAN (SD-WAN) and infrastructure-as-code can help replicate firewall rules, routing, and segmentation across sites.

5. **Plan for latency and bandwidth**: Moving data between clouds and your data center takes time and money. Place workloads and data close to each other whenever possible.

Exam Tip #53

Be ready to match deployment models to their characteristics and identify when hybrid or multi-cloud makes sense. The exam may present scenarios involving data sovereignty, burst workloads, or regulatory compliance and ask which model fits best.

Cloud Networking and Virtual Integration

Deploying VMs in the cloud is only half the story; those VMs need to communicate with one another, with the Internet and with your on-premises networks. **Cloud networking** provides virtualized equivalents of routers, switches, and firewalls, along with services like DNS and load balancing. Getting networking right is critical for performance, security, and cost control.

Use virtual CPU (vCPU) overcommit ratios (e.g., 4:1) judiciously to maximize utilization without degrading performance. Implement virtual firewalls or microsegmentation (e.g., VMware NSX, Azure vNet rules) to isolate virtual machines on the same host or network segment.

Core Components of Cloud Networking

1. **Virtual Private Cloud (VPC)/Virtual Network (VNet)**: A logically isolated slice of the provider's network where you can define subnets, route tables, DHCP options, and IP address ranges. VPCs in AWS and VNets in Azure act like your own data center inside the cloud.

2. **Subnets**: Segments within a VPC that divide resources into functional or security groups (e.g., public web servers, application servers, and database servers). Subnets can span multiple availability zones for redundancy.

3. **Gateways**: Devices that connect your VPC to other networks. An **Internet gateway** provides outbound access to the Internet for public subnets. A **VPN gateway** or **Cloud VPN** creates an IPsec tunnel between your on-premises environment and the cloud. **Direct Connect**, **ExpressRoute,** or **Dedicated Interconnect** offer high-bandwidth private links.

4. **NAT Gateway/NAT Instance**: Network address translation devices that allow instances in private subnets to initiate outbound connections while remaining unreachable from the Internet. Managed NAT gateways simplify scaling and availability.

5. **Load balancers**: Distribute traffic across multiple instances to improve availability and performance. Cloud providers offer **layer 4 (TCP/UDP)** and **layer 7 (HTTP/HTTPS)** load balancers, often with automatic health checks and SSL termination.

6. **DNS and service discovery** Services like Amazon Route 53, Azure DNS, and Google Cloud DNS provide domain name resolution and routing policies such as weighted load balancing or latency-based routing. Service discovery tools (e.g., AWS Cloud Map, Consul) register and locate microservice endpoints dynamically.

7. **Security controls: Security groups** act as stateful instance-level firewalls. **Network ACLs** are stateless filters at the subnet boundary. Both enforce least-privilege by restricting inbound and outbound traffic. Advanced services like AWS Transit Gateway or Azure Virtual WAN simplify routing and segmentation across multiple VPCs and VPNs.

Virtual Networking Beyond the Basics

Cloud providers also support more complex networking scenarios:

1. **Peering** connects VPCs across accounts or regions, enabling private communication without traversing the public Internet.

2. **VPC endpoints** allow private connections from your VPC to managed smanagelike S3 or DynamoDB, eliminating the need for a public IP.

3. **Overlay networks and service meshes**, such as Istio and Linkerd, provide traffic management, encryption, and observability for microservices. They abstract the network layer even further and integrate with orchestration platforms like Kubernetes.

4. **Software-defined WAN (SD-WAN)** technologies extend your network into the cloud with centralized control, dynamic path selection, and improved performance for SaaS applications.

Real-World Example: Building a Secure Web Application

You're tasked with deploying a customer-facing web application in the cloud. You create a VPC with three subnets: a **public subnet** for the load balancer, a **private subnet** for the web server instances, and another **private subnet** for the database. Security groups restrict traffic so that only the load balancer can talk to the web servers on port 443 and only the web servers can talk to the database on port 3306. A site-to-site VPN connects the VPC to your data center so internal administrators can manage the environment. Later you enable **VPC Flow Logs** to capture metadata about network traffic and send it to your SIEM for analysis. This architecture provides defense-in-depth while allowing you to scale out web servers to handle peak demand.

Best Practices for Cloud Networking

For east-west traffic inside the environment, microsegmentation or virtual firewalls (e.g., NSX) can isolate VMs even when they share the same host or network segment.

1. **Segment your network**: Use separate subnets and security groups for different tiers (web, app, database) and restrict traffic between them. Avoid placing database servers in public subnets.

2. **Minimize public exposure**: Use NAT gateways, VPC endpoints and bastion hosts to avoid giving instances public IP addresses unless absolutely necessary.

3. **Monitor and log traffic**: Enable flow logs, DNS query logs and IDS/IPS services. Integrate these logs with your monitoring and alerting systems.

4. **Automate network provisioning**: Treat network infrastructure as code. Tools like Terraform, AWS CloudFormation, and Azure Resource Manager can define VPCs, subnets, security groups, and gateways declaratively.

5. **Plan for resilience**: Deploy resources across multiple availability zones or regions. Use load balancers and auto scaling groups to redistribute traffic during failures. Test failover scenarios regularly.

Exam Tip #54

The exam will expect you to identify components like VPCs, subnets, VPN gateways, NAT devices, and security groups and understand how they fit together. Be ready to design a simple cloud network for a given scenario and explain how to secure and monitor it.

Cloud Security and Compliance Considerations

Moving workloads to the cloud doesn't absolve you of security and compliance responsibilities. In fact, the **shared responsibility model** means you must be crystal clear about what the provider does and what you must do. Cloud security is a combination of good architectural choices, robust identity and access management, strong encryption, continuous monitoring, and adherence to regulatory standards.

Use Type 1 hypervisors in production. Their direct access to hardware yields better performance and security than hosted solutions. Distinguish Type 1 hypervisors, used in enterprise environments for performance/security, from Type 2 (hosted) hypervisors such as VirtualBox or VMware Workstation.

Shared Responsibility Model

The division of labor varies by service model:

1. In **IaaS**, the provider secures the facilities, physical servers, networking, and hypervisor. You secure the OS, applications, and data, configure firewalls and manage identities.

2. In **PaaS**, the provider also secures the runtime and middleware, leaving you to secure your code and data.

3. In **SaaS**, the provider handles nearly everything, but you're still responsible for user access, data classification, and regulatory compliance.

Understanding where the provider's responsibility ends and yours begins is critical to avoid gaps.

Identity and Access Management (IAM)

Central to cloud security is **IAM**, which controls who can access what. Best practices include

1. **Least privilege**: Grant users and applications only the permissions they need to perform their tasks. Review roles regularly and remove unnecessary access.

2. **Multi-factor authentication (MFA)**: Require MFA for console and API access to reduce the risk of credential compromise.

3. **Role-based access control (RBAC)** and **attribute-based access control (ABAC)**: Assign permissions based on job function or resource attributes rather than individual accounts.

4. **Federated identity**: Integrate cloud IAM with your corporate directory (e.g., via SAML or OIDC) so users can use single sign-on and your identity provider remains the source of truth.

Data Protection and Encryption

Protecting data at rest and in transit is non-negotiable. Key recommendations include

1. **Encryption at rest**: Use provider-supplied key management services (e.g., AWS KMS, Azure Key Vault) or bring your own keys to encrypt volumes, object storage, and databases. Regularly rotate keys and restrict who can access them.

2. **Encryption in transit**: Enforce HTTPS/TLS for web traffic, SSH or VPNs for administrative access and secure protocols like SFTP for file transfers. For internal service communications, use service meshes or mutual TLS.

3. **Tokenization and masking**: For highly sensitive data (e.g., payment card information), consider tokenization or masking to remove direct identifiers.

Monitoring, Logging, and Incident Response

1. **Enable logging** on to all cloud resources. Services like AWS CloudTrail, Azure Activity Log, and Google Cloud Audit Logs capture API calls and changes to the environment. VPC Flow Logs and firewall logs reveal network activity.

2. **Centralize logs** in to a SIEM or log analytics platform to correlate events across services. Use alerting rules to flag suspicious patterns such as repeated failed logins or sudden spikes in data egress.

3. **Implement intrusion detection and prevention**: Cloud-native services (e.g., AWS GuardDuty, Azure Defender) and third-party tools analyze traffic and logs for indicators of compromise.

4. **Develop an incident response plan** tailored to the cloud. Define roles, communication channels and playbooks for common scenarios like credential leaks or DDOS attacks. Practice the plan through tabletop exercises.

Compliance and Governance

Depending on your industry and geography, you may need to adhere to regulations such as **HIPAA** (healthcare), **PCI-DSS** (payment card), **GDPR** (European privacy), **FedRAMP** (US government) or **ISO/IEC 27001**. Achieving compliance in the cloud involves

1. **Choosing compliant services**: Many providers offer specific regions or service tiers certified for certain standards.

2. **Documenting controls and processes**: Maintain evidence of encryption, access controls, audits, and backups. Cloud providers often provide compliance reports and attestation frameworks to simplify this.

3. **Performing regular audits and assessments**: Use tools like AWS Config, Azure Policy, or third-party compliance scanners to check your environment against defined policies.

4. **Embracing security frameworks**: Follow best practices outlined in frameworks such as the **NIST Cybersecurity Framework**, **CIS Controls**, or **CSA Cloud Controls Matrix**.

Real-World Example: Securing a Serverless Application

A start-up builds an event-driven application using AWS Lambda and DynamoDB. Developers enable encryption at rest on all DynamoDB tables, enforce TLS for API Gateway endpoints and use IAM roles with least-privileged policies for each function. CloudTrail and CloudWatch Logs send data to a managed SIEM, which alerts on anomalous behavior. Regular security reviews ensure that new features adhere to the company's compliance requirements for handling customer information. When auditors review the environment, they find comprehensive documentation of controls and a clear separation of duties between the provider and the customer.

Best Practices for Cloud Security and Compliance

1. **Know your responsibilities**: Map out what you manage vs. what the provider manages. Don't assume the provider secures your applications or data.

2. **Apply defense-in-depth**: Layer security controls (firewalls, security groups, IAM policies, encryption) to mitigate the impact of any single failure.

3. **Automate security**: Use templates and policy-as-code to ensure that security is baked into every deployment. Tools like AWS Security Hub and Azure Security Center can continuously audit your environment.

4. **Educate your teams**: Security is everyone's responsibility. Provide training on security coding, data handling, and incident reporting.

5. **Stay current on threats and updates**: Cloud providers rapidly release new features and security advisories. Subscribe to bulletins and participate in cloud user groups to keep your knowledge fresh.

Exam Tip #55

Be prepared for questions on the shared responsibility model, IAM best practices, encryption options, and compliance standards. The exam may also present a scenario involving a breach or misconfiguration and ask which logging service or response procedure you should use.

Chapter Summary

Virtualization and cloud computing are cornerstones of modern IT, transforming how organizations deploy, scale, and secure their applications. You learned that virtualization decouples workloads from hardware, enabling consolidation, portability, and high availability through features like live migration and distributed resource scheduling. Hypervisors come in two flavors—bare-metal and hosted—and support technologies such as paravirtualized drivers, snapshots, virtual switches, and storage virtualization.

Building on virtualization, cloud service models—IaaS, PaaS, SaaS, FaaS, and CaaS—offer increasing levels of abstraction. Choosing the right model depends on how much control you need versus how much operational burden you're willing to offload. Deployment models public, private, hybrid, community, and multi-cloud—determine where resources live and who shares them. Matching the model to your risk, compliance, and performance requirements is key.

You explored cloud networking components like VPCs, subnets, gateways, NAT devices, load balancers, and DNS, and saw how they work together to build secure and scalable architectures. You also learned to use network segmentation, automation and monitoring to maintain visibility and control. Security and compliance were examined through the lens of the shared responsibility model, IAM best practices, encryption, logging, incident response, and regulatory frameworks.

Armed with this knowledge, you're ready to design virtualization solutions, select appropriate cloud services, architect resilient networks, and implement robust security in any environment. Whether you're consolidating servers, deploying a serverless app, or negotiating a multi-cloud strategy, the principles covered here will help you deliver reliable and secure services at scale.

CHAPTER 11

Network Troubleshooting Scenarios

No matter how well you design and secure your network, things will go wrong. Cables get unplugged, DHCP servers run out of leases, wireless clients roam into dead zones and firmware updates introduce new problems. When outages happen, the ability to troubleshoot quickly and methodically is what separates seasoned network professionals from the panicked masses. In this chapter, we'll build on the monitoring and logging practices you learned earlier to diagnose and resolve a wide range of wired and wireless issues.

We'll start by reviewing structured troubleshooting frameworks and then dive into common wireless problems such as weak signals, interference, and roaming hiccups. From there we'll tackle wired connectivity and performance issues like IP conflicts, duplex mismatches, and DNS failures. You'll learn how to interpret logs, correlate symptoms with root causes, and choose the right tool for the job. Along the way, we'll share real-world war stories, best practices, and exam tips so you're prepared for both the field and the certification exam.

© Kodi A. Cochran 2026

K. A. Cochran, *CompTIA Network+ (N10-009) Certification Companion*, Certification Study Companion Series, https://doi.org/10.1007/979-8-8688-2341-1_11

A Structured Approach to Troubleshooting

Troubleshooting isn't guesswork; it's a disciplined process. Without a framework, you risk chasing red herrings, making unnecessary changes and fixing the wrong problem. The **CompTIA six-step process** is a widely adopted methodology for tackling issues systematically. Each step builds on the previous one and helps ensure you understand the problem before you start replacing hardware or reconfiguring routers.

Before relocating hardware or access points, verify that client devices are not misconfigured or limited by power-saving settings. Implement band steering to shift capable clients to 5 GHz or 6 GHz and alleviate 2.4 GHz congestion. Troubleshoot poor roaming by enabling band steering, client load balancing, and ensuring legacy clients support 802.11k/v/r.

The Six-Step Troubleshooting Process

1. **Identify the problem:** Start by gathering as much information as you can. Ask the user what they were doing when the problem occurred, note error messages, and check indicator lights. Use commands like ping, ipconfig (or ifconfig on Linux), and netstat to confirm connectivity and see open ports. Don't forget to document symptoms such as "Cannot access internal HR portal" or "Wireless network drops when moving between conference rooms."

2. **Establish a theory of probable causes:** Based on the evidence collected, hypothesize what might be wrong. Consider layers of the OSI model: Is it a physical issue (cable, NIC, Wi-Fi radio), a network layer issue (routing, DHCP, DNS), or an application issue (server misconfiguration)? Generate more than one possible cause.

3. **Test the theory to determine the cause:** Use tools and experiments to confirm or refute your theories. Swap cables, reboot the client, move closer to the access point or roll back recent configuration changes. Be deliberate: change only one variable at a time so you can isolate the effect.

4. **Establish a plan of action and identify potential effects:** Once you're confident in the cause, decide how to fix it. Consider business impact, potential side effects, and whether you need approval from change control. For example, updating firmware on a production router should be scheduled, while replacing a patch cord can be done immediately. Always have a back-out plan.

5. **Implement the solution or escalation:** Apply the fix within your authority. If the solution is outside your remit—like replacing a core switch—escalate to the appropriate team. Use maintenance windows and communicate with stakeholders when service interruptions are expected.

6. **Verify full system functionality and implement preventative measures:** After applying the fix, verify that not only the original issue but all related services are working. Run tests, monitor logs, and ask users to confirm. Then implement measures to prevent recurrence: apply patches, update documentation, adjust monitoring thresholds, or schedule training.

7. **Document findings, actions, and outcomes:** Good documentation turns individual troubleshooting experiences into organizational knowledge. Record what went wrong, what you discovered, how you resolved it, and any follow-up actions. Ticketing systems and knowledge bases help others solve similar issues faster.

Although often called a six-step process, the last step—documentation—is sometimes considered implicit. We include it here to emphasize its importance.

Exam Tip #56

You should be able to recite the six (or seven) steps in order and match troubleshooting actions to the appropriate step. The exam may present a scenario and ask which step you're currently performing or what you should do next.

Real-World Example: The Forgotten Patch Cord

During a building renovation, a contractor accidentally pulls an Ethernet cable out of a patch panel. Several offices lose connectivity. The help desk receives calls and begins by identifying the scope: users can't reach any network resource. A network map reveals all affected jacks terminate on the same switch port. The technician visits the IDF (Intermediate Distribution Frame) and discovers the loose cable. Reconnecting it restores service, and a note is added to the building project plan to protect cabling during construction.

Best Practices for Structured Troubleshooting

1. **Stay calm and methodical:** Users may be frustrated, but panic leads to sloppy troubleshooting. Follow the process even under pressure.

2. **Communicate clearly:** Explain what you're doing and when users can expect updates. Transparency builds trust.

3. **Leverage history:** Review past incidents for similar symptoms. Networks often repeat themselves.

4. **Use the right tool for the job:** Cable testers, Wi-Fi analyzers, protocol analyzers, and log aggregators each have their place. Don't over-rely on a single tool.

5. **Follow change control:** Even "simple" fixes can have unintended consequences. When in doubt, schedule changes and seek approval.

Troubleshooting Wireless Networks

Wireless networks add a layer of complexity to troubleshooting because RF signals are invisible and subject to environmental factors. A Wi-Fi issue could stem from channel interference, physical obstructions, client configuration, or a misbehaving access point. Let's explore common wireless problems and how to solve them.

Weak Signal Strength and Dead Zones

A low signal-to-noise ratio (SNR) manifests as slow speeds, dropped connections, and difficulty associating to the SSID. Causes and solutions include

1. **Distance from the access point:** The further away you are, the weaker the signal. Add more APs, reposition them, or use higher-gain antennas to ensure coverage.

2. **Physical obstructions:** Brick walls, metal shelves, elevator shafts, and even water (including human bodies) attenuate RF signals. Conduct a site survey to map dead zones and adjust AP placement or power levels accordingly.

3. **Antenna orientation and type:** Omni-directional antennas radiate in all directions; directional antennas focus energy into a beam. Ensure antennas are oriented correctly and consider swapping for higher-gain models in challenging areas.

4. **Client device issues:** Older laptops or phones may have less sensitive Wi-Fi adapters. Updating drivers or using external adapters can improve reception.

Interference and Channel Planning

The unlicensed nature of Wi-Fi bands means you share spectrum with microwaves, cordless phones, Bluetooth devices, and neighboring networks. Symptoms include intermittent drops, low throughput, and poor VoIP quality. Mitigation strategies are as follow:

1. **Choose the right band:** The 2.4 GHz band has only three non-overlapping channels (1, 6, and 11) and is crowded. The 5 GHz band offers many more channels and typically less interference. The newer 6 GHz band (Wi-Fi 6E) provides even more spectrum.

2. **Perform a spectrum analysis:** Use tools like Wi-Fi analyzers or spectrum analyzers to visualize channel utilization and identify sources of interference. Adjust channel assignments to avoid co-channel and adjacent-channel interference. Perform periodic RF heatmaps using tools like Ekahau or NetSpot to identify coverage gaps after changes in the environment.

3. **Reduce channel width:** Wider channels (40 MHz, 80 MHz) offer higher throughput but are more susceptible to interference. In congested areas, narrower channels may provide better reliability.

4. **Separate SSIDs by purpose:** Isolate guest Wi-Fi on its own channel or band to prevent guests from saturating the same channel as critical business devices.

5. **Manage transmit power:** Excessive AP power can create hidden node problems where clients can hear the AP but not each other. Balance power to minimize overlaps while maintaining coverage.

Hidden SSIDs and Association Issues

When a client can't see an SSID or fails to authenticate, consider these factors:

1. **Hidden SSIDs:** Some administrators disable SSID broadcast for security. Clients must manually configure the SSID and security settings. Hidden SSIDs provide little security benefit and can hinder connectivity. A better practice is to broadcast the SSID and rely on WPA2/WPA3 and 802.1X for security. Prefer strong security (e.g., WPA2/WPA3) over hiding SSIDs; do not rely on disabling SSID broadcasts for protection.

2. **Mismatched security settings:** A client configured for WPA3 cannot connect to an AP running WPA2 only. Ensure encryption and authentication settings match on both sides.

3. **RADIUS or captive portal issues:** Enterprise Wi-Fi often uses RADIUS servers to authenticate users. If the RADIUS server is unreachable or certificates have expired, clients will fail to authenticate. Check logs on both the AP and the RADIUS server.

4. **MAC filtering:** Some networks restrict access by MAC address. Confirm that the client's MAC is permitted.

5. **Device configuration:** Mistyped passwords, disabled Wi-Fi adapters, or outdated firmware can all prevent association.

Conduct post-mortems for recurring or escalated issues and document lessons learned in a knowledge base for faster resolution in the future.

Roaming and Handoff Problems

As users move around a building, their devices should smoothly roam between access points. If clients disconnect or experience drops while walking, consider these causes:

1. **Inconsistent SSID and security configuration across Aps:** All APs in the same roaming domain should broadcast the same SSID and support the same encryption standards. Otherwise, clients will treat them as different networks.

2. **Sticky clients:** Some devices cling to an AP even when its signal has become weak. Enabling aggressive roaming on clients or using features like 802.11k (Neighbor Reports) and 802.11v (BSS transition) helps devices make smarter roaming decisions.

3. **Improper signal threshold settings:** APs often have settings that determine when a client should be handed off. Adjust these thresholds to encourage handoff before the signal becomes unusable.

4. **Fast transition (802.11r):** Implementing fast roaming protocols reduces authentication delays when moving between APs, improving experience for VoIP and video.

Real-World Example: The Noisy Lunchroom

Employees complain that Wi-Fi in the company cafeteria drops around lunchtime. A spectrum scan reveals that a commercial microwave oven operates on 2.4 GHz and generates bursts of interference. Moving the AP to the 5 GHz band and lowering the microwave's power setting (or replacing it with a model that leaks less RF) resolves the problem.

Best Practices for Wireless Troubleshooting

1. **Perform regular site surveys:** Use heatmap tools to visualize coverage and adjust AP placement, channel assignments, and power levels.

2. **Standardize security and SSID settings:** Consistency across APs ensures seamless roaming and reduces authentication errors.

3. **Monitor client counts and utilization:** An overloaded AP will drop connections. Load balance clients across APs or add more capacity.

4. **Keep firmware updated:** Vendors frequently release bug fixes and improvements for wireless controllers and APs.

5. **Plan for density:** Conference rooms, auditoriums, and lobbies require more APs and careful channel planning. Use directional antennas or beamforming to concentrate signals where people gather.

Exam Tip #57

Expect the exam to present scenarios involving SSID visibility, interference, security mismatches, and roaming issues. Know which settings to check on both the client and the AP and which diagnostic tools (spectrum analyzers, Wi-Fi analyzers, controller logs) to use.

Diagnosing Wired Connectivity and Performance Problems

Investigate logs for NIC resets, DHCP negotiation failures, or DNS issues when diagnosing connectivity problems. While wireless often draws headlines, most enterprise infrastructure relies on wired connections. When desktops can't access a server or a VoIP phone has choppy audio, the cause might be a simple cable issue or a complex routing problem. Let's explore common symptoms, their likely causes, and how to resolve them.

No Connectivity

A device can't reach any local or Internet resources. Troubleshoot as follows:

1. **Physical layer first:** Check that the cable is firmly seated and not damaged. Inspect patch panels and wall jacks. Use a cable tester or tone generator to verify continuity.

2. **Link status:** Examine NIC link lights. A dark light indicates no electrical signal; check the switch port status. Amber or flashing lights may signal errors or negotiation problems.

3. **Layer 3 settings:** Verify that the device has a valid IP address, subnet mask, and default gateway. If it uses DHCP, ensure the server is reachable and has available leases.

4. **Default gateway reachability:** Can the device ping the default gateway? If not, there may be a switch configuration issue or a routing problem further upstream.

5. **Security controls:** Firewalls or NAC (Network Access Control) systems may block a device based on MAC address or posture. Check the logs.

Check power-over-Ethernet (PoE) budgets and class compatibility to avoid intermittent resets of IP phones and APs.

Intermittent Connectivity

Sporadic drops can be maddening. Consider these possibilities:

1. **Damaged or poorly terminated cables:** A single broken wire can cause packets to drop intermittently. Replace suspect cables and verify termination quality.

2. **Overheating equipment:** Switches and routers with failing fans may overheat and throttle or reboot. Check environmental sensors and ensure proper ventilation.

3. **EMI (Electromagnetic Interference):** Cables run near fluorescent lights, motors, or large transformers can pick up noise. Use shielded cables (STP) or reroute away from interference sources.

4. **Spanning Tree Protocol (STP) recalculations:** If there's a Layer 2 loop or a port flapping, STP may frequently reconverge, causing momentary network pauses. Check switch logs and topology.

5. **Wireless bridging:** Some "wired" links are actually wireless bridges (e.g., point-to-point Wi-Fi). Weather, interference, or alignment issues can impact these links.

Slow Speeds and Performance Bottlenecks

Sluggish file transfers or lagging applications often point to congestion or misconfiguration:

1. **Duplex mismatch:** When one end of a link is set to full duplex and the other to half duplex, collisions and CRC errors occur. Auto-negotiation usually prevents mismatches but manually set ports can cause problems. Align settings on both sides.

2. **Bandwidth saturation:** A user streaming high-definition video can consume significant bandwidth. Use network monitoring to identify top talkers and implement QoS or rate limiting.

3. **Broadcast storms:** Excessive broadcast traffic (e.g., from a rogue DHCP server or misconfigured device) can overwhelm the network. Use switch counters and packet captures to isolate the source.

4. **Oversubscription:** If many devices share uplinks to the core switch, aggregated traffic may exceed link capacity. Upgrade uplinks or restructure the topology.

5. **QoS misconfigurations:** Quality-of-service policies that prioritize or police traffic incorrectly can throttle legitimate traffic. Review QoS settings and ensure they match business requirements.

   - Apply port security, DHCP snooping, and BPDU Guard on access switches to prevent rogue devices and loops.

6. **Fragmentation and MTU issues:** Mismatched maximum transmission units can cause

fragmentation and retransmissions. Ensure MTU sizes are consistent end to end, especially when VPNs or tunnels are involved. Address MTU mismatches, especially in VPNs or tunnels, by using Path MTU Discovery or adjusting TCP MSS.

IP Address and DHCP Issues

When a device has no IP address or an unexpected one

1. **No lease from DHCP:** The DHCP server may be down or not reachable. Check server status and confirm VLANs and scopes are correct.

2. **APIPA addresses:** Windows devices assign a 169.254.x.x address when they cannot reach a DHCP server. This indicates a network communication problem.

3. **IP conflicts:** Two devices may have been statically assigned the same IP or a rogue DHCP server may be handing out addresses outside your scope. Identify duplicates with arp -a and DHCP logs.

4. **Incorrect subnet or gateway:** A misconfigured subnet mask or default gateway prevents communication outside the local segment.

DNS and Name Resolution Problems

When users can access IP addresses but not hostnames

1. **Wrong DNS server:** Ensure DHCP options or static settings point to the correct DNS server(s). Using a public DNS resolver may bypass internal name records.

2. **Stale DNS records:** DNS caches or TTL settings may return outdated information. Flush client caches (ipconfig/flushdns) and restart the DNS service.

3. **Zone configuration errors:** Missing or incorrect A, CNAME, or PTR records can cause lookups to fail. Check your DNS zone files.

4. **DNS server outages:** Primary DNS may be down; verify that secondary servers are configured and reachable.

Real-World Example: The Phantom DHCP Server

Users across multiple floors start receiving wrong IP addresses. A trace reveals a consumer Wi-Fi router plugged into the corporate LAN, handing out 192.168.0.x addresses. The rogue DHCP server is located and removed, and port security is enabled on access switches to prevent unauthorized devices from connecting. Enable DHCP snooping on access switches and explicitly define trusted ports to prevent rogue servers.

Best Practices for Wired Troubleshooting

1. **Always start with Layer 1:** Inspect cables and connectors before diving into complex configurations.

2. **Use link-local tests:** Test connectivity to the default gateway first, then expand outward. Traceroute helps locate where connectivity breaks down.

3. **Keep diagrams up-to-date:** Accurate network maps make it easier to trace a path and identify potential failure points.

4. **Segment your network:** Proper VLAN design and segmentation reduce the blast radius of broadcast storms, loops, or misconfigured devices.

5. **Implement change control:** Unexpected outages often correlate with recent changes. Logging and reviewing changes aids troubleshooting.

Exam Tip #58

Be ready to diagnose symptoms like "I can't reach the Internet but can ping the gateway" or "My laptop keeps getting a 169.254 address." Know which commands to run (ping, tracert, arp, netstat, nslookup) and what their outputs mean.

Key Log Sources

Regularly audit log sources to ensure critical components (DNS, VPN gateways, cloud APIs) are not omitted. Logs are invaluable detectives. By examining system and application logs, you can spot patterns, correlate events, and uncover the root of many problems. With so many devices generating logs, centralizing collection and analysis is essential.

1. **Operating system logs:** Windows Event Viewer and Linux syslog files contain messages about hardware drivers, services, authentication, and more.

2. **Network device logs:** Routers, switches, firewalls, and wireless controllers often export logs via **Syslog**. These logs record interface status changes,

routing updates, NAT translations, and blocked connections. Send SNMP traps and Syslog messages to a centralized server for proactive monitoring of device status changes.

3. **Security appliances and SIEMs:** Intrusion detection systems, Unified Threat Management (UTM) devices, and SIEM platforms correlate events from across the network. They can spot brute-force attempts, malware outbreaks, or data exfiltration.

4. **Application logs:** Web servers, database servers, and custom applications produce logs that reveal authentication failures, query errors, and performance bottlenecks. Monitor application logs for HTTP 4xx/5xx codes, response latency, and session timeouts in web applications.

Validate Extensible Authentication Protocol (EAP) method compatibility between clients and RADIUS servers to prevent silent failures.

Reading Between the Lines

Interpreting logs requires context. A single "interface down" message may not be significant if it coincides with scheduled maintenance, but multiple flaps across different devices could indicate a larger issue. Tips for analysis are as follow:

1. **Correlate across layers:** A high CPU alert on a router followed by BGP session drops suggests the router is overwhelmed. Align timestamps across logs using a synchronized NTP server.

2. **Look for patterns:** Repeated authentication failures from the same IP might signal a brute-force attack.

Frequent DHCP lease declines could indicate a conflict.

3. **Understand severity levels:** Syslog messages have severities from 0 (emergency) to 7 (debug). Focus on critical, alert, and error messages first.

4. **Use search and filtering:** SIEMs allow you to query logs for specific fields (e.g., destination port 3389) or time ranges. Learn to write filters that narrow down noise.

5. **Leverage dashboards and alerts:** Visualizations help you spot outliers. Configure alerts for anomalies like a surge in DNS queries or repeated failed logins.

Real-World Example: Unraveling a Broadcast Storm

Users report slow network performance and occasional timeouts. The NOC notices a spike in broadcast traffic. Syslog from multiple switches show constant STP topology changes. Logs point to a recently installed unmanaged switch creating a loop. After removing the offending device and ensuring all access switches have spanning tree enabled, broadcast traffic returns to normal. Utilize SIEM correlation and anomaly detection to identify slow-moving attacks that signature-based tools might otherwise miss.

Best Practices for Log Management

1. **Centralize and normalize:** Use log collectors like Graylog, Logstash, or a managed SIEM to bring logs into a common format and store them centrally.

2. **Set retention policies:** Balance storage costs with forensic needs. Some compliance standards require keeping logs for years.

3. **Encrypt logs in transit and at rest:** Protect sensitive information and prevent tampering.

4. **Automate alerts:** Define thresholds for CPU, memory, disk, and traffic anomalies. Tie alerts into incident response workflows.

5. **Review regularly:** Threats evolve. Adjust your logging and alerting rules based on new attack techniques and business priorities.

Exam Tip #59

The exam may show you a snippet of a log and ask what the problem is. Know where to find key information in Windows Event Viewer, Syslog severity codes, and common firewall or wireless controller messages.

Troubleshooting Tools and Techniques

1. Effective troubleshooting relies on the right tools. While we've mentioned many already, it's useful to categorize.

- **Utilities:** Ping tests reachability and round-trip time; tracert/traceroute reveals the path packets take; arp displays the ARP cache; netstat lists open connections; ipconfig and ifconfig show interface configuration; nslookup and dig query DNS; tshark and tcpdump capture traffic.

2. **GUI analyzers: Wireshark** decodes packets to identify application delays, retransmissions, and protocol errors. **Nmap** scans networks to discover hosts and open ports. **SolarWinds**, **PRTG,** and **Zabbix** provide visual dashboards and alerting.

3. **Cable testers and certifiers:** Validate copper and fiber cables, identify shorts, splits, and crosstalk. **Tone generators** and **probe kits** help locate cables behind walls. **Optical time-domain reflectometers (OTDRs)** diagnose fiber breaks.

4. **Wireless analyzers:** Handheld or app-based tools display signal strength, channel usage, and interference sources. **Spectrum analyzers** reveal non-Wi-Fi devices emitting RF energy.

5. **Performance testing tools: iPerf** measures throughput, latency, and jitter between two endpoints. **Speedtest** and **PathPing** (a Windows tool) combine ping and traceroute to show packet loss per hop.

6. **Remote diagnostics: SNMP** for polling device stats, **Syslog** for remote logging, and **Secure Shell (SSH)** for CLI access to network devices.

Best Practices for Using Tools

1. **Use baseline data:** Without a baseline, it's hard to know if latency is abnormal. Collect performance data during normal operation for comparison.

2. **Capture before you change:** Record symptoms and metrics before adjusting. This makes it easier to evaluate the impact of your fix.

3. **Respect privacy and policy:** Packet captures can contain sensitive data. Ensure you have authorization and mask or discard confidential payloads.

4. **Correlate multiple sources:** Don't rely on one tool. Combine logs, SNMP counters, and packet captures to build a complete picture.

5. **Stay current:** Update your troubleshooting toolkit and skills regularly. New protocols and technologies introduce new tools and considerations.

Exam Tip #60

Be familiar with the purpose and basic usage of troubleshooting tools. The exam may ask which tool you'd use to verify DNS resolution, test throughput, or identify a cabling fault.

Chapter Summary

This chapter equipped you with a toolkit for diagnosing and resolving network problems. We began with a structured troubleshooting methodology that emphasizes gathering information, forming and testing theories, planning actions, implementing fixes, verifying results, and documenting outcomes. Following a process ensures you address the root cause rather than chasing symptoms.

Wireless networks bring their own challenges. You learned how distance, obstacles, interference, and security settings impact performance and how to remedy weak signals, hidden SSIDs, authentication issues, and roaming problems. Real-world scenarios like noisy lunchrooms illustrated the importance of spectrum analysis and channel planning. On the wired side, we explored connectivity, performance, DHCP, DNS, and cabling issues. You discovered how duplex mismatches, broadcast storms, rogue DHCP servers, and misconfigured gateways can break communications. Best practices emphasized starting at the physical layer, keeping diagrams current and adhering to change control.

Interpreting logs and correlating symptoms across layers is key to identifying root causes. We reviewed log sources, severity levels and analysis techniques, then summarized the most useful troubleshooting tools—from command-line utilities and packet analyzers to cable certifiers and wireless scanners. A reference table brought the chapter's concepts together for quick problem-to-solution mapping.

As you continue your journey in networking, remember that patience, attention to detail, and clear documentation will serve you well. When users report "the network is down," you now have the mindset and resources to get them back online quickly and prevent the issue from recurring.

CHAPTER 12

Physical Security and Forensics

Network security is often discussed in terms of firewalls, encryption algorithms, IPS signatures, and authentication technologies. Yet all of these tools share a common weakness: no one can protect systems if an attacker is able to physically access the equipment. A single open door, a distracted employee, or an unmonitored server room can undermine even the most sophisticated security design. Physical security is the first and most fundamental layer of defense. Without it, confidentiality, integrity, and availability cannot be guaranteed—and forensic evidence cannot be preserved when something goes wrong.

This chapter reinforces the foundation of real-world security by examining how organizations secure buildings, rooms, racks, cables, and hardware. It explains how layered physical controls deter, detect, and delay intruders, and how procedural safeguards support consistent enforcement. After establishing the physical side of protection, the chapter transitions into network forensics—the discipline of collecting, preserving, analyzing, and securing evidence from systems, logs, and network traffic.

© Kodi A. Cochran 2026
K. A. Cochran, *CompTIA Network+ (N10-009) Certification Companion,*
Certification Study Companion Series, https://doi.org/10.1007/979-8-8688-2341-1_12

Through practical examples, structured best practices, and exam-oriented insights, you will learn what effective physical security looks like, how hardware should be defended against tampering, and how forensic processes maintain the integrity of evidence throughout an investigation. These concepts are essential for real environments and directly tested on the Network+ exam.

Building a Layered Physical Defense

Physical security is most effective when implemented as a series of layered controls rather than reliance on a single device or mechanism. No single safeguard is perfect; instead, each layer should work together to determine, detect, and delay unauthorized access long enough for staff or automated systems to respond. Because IT infrastructure is distributed across server rooms, network closets, office floors, and shared spaces, physical security must address equipment at every location—not just in the data center.

Perimeter and Facility Controls

The perimeter defines the outermost protective boundary of a secure installation. Controls at this layer establish the first line of defense and set clear expectations for anyone approaching the facility. By integrating physical barriers, lighting, and human oversight, an organization can effectively deter, detect, and delay intruders.

Fencing and Barriers

Chain-link fencing, bollards, concrete planters, and controlled-entry gates help prevent unauthorized access and vehicle intrusion. Fencing should be high enough and anchored well enough to prevent simple climbing or cutting. Bollards protect entrances and critical exterior walls from vehicle ramming attacks and accidental collisions.

Lighting and Visibility

Effective exterior lighting is one of the simplest yet most important deterrents. Bright, consistent lighting around parking areas, walkways, and building entrances discourages intruders and improves camera image quality. Motion-activated lighting adds an element of surprise and signals movement to monitoring staff.

Security Personnel

Guards stationed at entrances or patrolling the perimeter provide human judgment, verification, and escalation capabilities. Many high-security facilities employ 24/7 on-site personnel, supported by a remote security operations center (SOC) that monitors alarms and cameras.

Signage

Clear signage reinforces legal boundaries. Signs indicating restricted access, camera surveillance, badge-required zones, and trespassing consequences serve as deterrents and provide legal notice for prosecution when incidents occur.

In regulated environments, signage should clearly mark restricted areas and align with organizational safety and accessibility requirements.

Controlling Access to Buildings and Rooms

Once inside the parking lot or fenced area, additional controls restrict access to the building itself and to sensitive interior spaces such as server rooms and network closets.

Badges and Key Cards

Electronic access systems use proximity cards, smart cards, or magnetic stripe badges. Access rights should be role-based, granting employees only the doors and hours they legitimately need. Deactivation of badges must occur immediately upon termination.

Biometric Scanners

Biometric fingerprints, palm veins, facial recognition, iris scanners provide stronger identity verification than badges alone. They reduce risks of badge theft, duplication, or sharing. Many organizations combine biometrics with PINs or cards for multi-factor authentication at sensitive entry points.

Mantraps and Turnstiles

A mantrap is a small chamber with two electronically controlled doors that cannot open simultaneously. This prevents tailgating (following someone through a door without authorization) and piggybacking (someone holding the door open for another person). Full-height turnstiles or revolving security doors are common in lobbies and large facilities.

Visitor Management

Visitors must be signed in, present valid identification, and wear temporary badges that expire after a defined time. Policies should require escorting visitors at all times. Visitor logs must be retained per security policy or compliance requirements.

Server Rooms and Network Closets

These areas require additional restrictions, including reinforced doors, unique access groups, and continuously maintained access logs. Door alarms should trigger when the door remains open longer than a set threshold. Only authorized technicians should have access, and all entries should be logged and reviewed.

Surveillance and Monitoring

Even with strong access controls, detection mechanisms are critical when unauthorized access attempts occur or when insider threats emerge.

CCTV Cameras

Modern IP-based CCTV provides high-resolution video, infrared illumination for low-light conditions, and pan-tilt-zoom capabilities. Cameras should cover entrances, hallways, server racks, and any areas where equipment or sensitive cabling is located. Overlapping angles reduce blind spots. Video retention policies should comply with legal and organizational requirements, and timestamps must be synchronized using NTP.

Motion Sensors and Alarms

Passive infrared (PIR) sensors, microwave sensors, glass-break detectors, and door contact sensors help detect unauthorized movement after hours. Alarms must send notifications directly to security staff or monitoring providers, with clear procedures for escalation.

Environmental Monitoring

Temperature, humidity, smoke, and water-leak sensors are essential. Excessive heat can indicate HVAC failure; water on the floor may reveal a pipe burst or sprinkler activation. Early detection protects equipment from irreversible damage.

Access Logs

Every badge swipe or biometric entry is recorded. Logs must be reviewed regularly to identify patterns such as off-hour access, repeated denied entries, or unexpected visits to restricted areas. When paired with video, access logs provide powerful investigative evidence.

Real-World Example: Tailgating and the Mantrap

During an after-hours maintenance window, a technician at a co-location data center held the door open for someone claiming to be a courier. Hours later, engineers discovered that a switch console cable had been moved, port security disabled, and unauthorized hardware connected. A review of CCTV footage showed the unauthorized individual had entered behind the technician.

Following the incident, the facility implemented a mantrap, required all personnel and vendors to badge in individually, and conducted additional security training. The incident reinforced a key truth: convenience and politeness cannot override physical security procedures.

Best Practices for Physical Access and Surveillance

Physical access systems (badges, mantraps, visitor management, and surveillance platforms) should generate time-stamped logs and feed into centralized logging or a SIEM when available.

1. Enforce a zero-trust approach to physical access.

2. Implement defense in depth across all facility layers.

3. Conduct regular physical penetration tests and audits.

4. Maintain accurate, secure logs of all access events.

5. Provide frequent security awareness training.

6. Periodically review camera placement, retention, and blind spots.

7. Require strict escorting procedures for all visitors.

Exam Tip #61

Know how to match physical security controls with the correct layer: perimeter (fences, lighting), building (badges, guards), restricted rooms (biometrics, mantraps), and equipment racks (locking cabinets). Expect scenarios involving tailgating, unauthorized access, or insufficient monitoring. Biometric data should be treated as sensitive: store templates securely (encrypted/hashed where applicable) and protect them using validated hardware or platform controls.

Protecting Devices and Hardware

Even inside secured rooms, hardware itself requires protection. A determined attacker with direct access to a device can bypass operating system controls using hardware keyloggers, bootable media, direct memory access, or physical theft. Environmental hazards—heat, fire, water—pose additional risks.

Tamper-Evident Seals and Intrusion Switches

Many servers include chassis intrusion detection switches that trigger alerts when a case is opened. Tamper-evident seals placed on screws, doors, and panels provide visual evidence of unauthorized access attempts. These mechanisms help detect both malicious activity and improper technician behavior.

BIOS/UEFI and TPM Protections

Strong BIOS/UEFI passwords prevent unauthorized users from modifying boot sequences, disabling security features, or performing firmware-level attacks. Secure Boot ensures only trusted, signed software loads at startup. Trusted Platform Modules (TPMs) store cryptographic keys and support full-disk encryption. Self-encrypting drives (SEDs) automatically lock when removed from the original system.

Drive and Port Locks

Chassis locks, rack security doors, and drive bay locks prevent physical removal of storage. USB port blockers deter unauthorized flash drives, and unused ports can be disabled via BIOS or endpoint management policies.

Cable Management

Leaving cables exposed or loosely routed increases risks of accidental disconnections and deliberate taps. Conduits, lockable cable trays, and secure patch panels help protect fiber and copper connections while maintaining organization.

Asset Management and Tracking

Asset tags, barcodes, or RFID labels help track equipment, detect unauthorized movement, and reconcile inventory. Pairing asset databases with network discovery tools ensures logical and physical records stay aligned.

Environmental and Redundancy Controls

Hardware failure often stems from environmental factors. Redundant systems and monitoring significantly reduce downtime.

UPS Units and Backup Generators

UPS devices provide immediate short-term power during outages, protect against voltage fluctuations, and allow servers to shut down gracefully. Generators support long-term continuity and must be tested regularly.

Redundant Power and Cooling

Redundant power supplies, power circuits, and cooling units eliminate single points of failure. Hot-aisle/cold-aisle containment optimizes airflow. Temperature and humidity sensors warn administrators of dangerous fluctuations.

Fire Suppression Systems

Clean agent systems like FM-200, Inergen, or Novec 1230 extinguish fires without damaging electronics. Fire suppression should be integrated with alarm systems and undergo routine testing.

Leak, Smoke, and Vibration Sensors

Early detection of leaks, smoke, or seismic activity helps prevent data loss and equipment damage.

Real-World Example: Stolen Backup Drives

A small business stored removable backup drives on an open shelf next to its server rack. During a burglary, thieves stole the drives, making full recovery impossible after a later ransomware event. The company responded by implementing encrypted off-site backups, securing removable media in a locked safe, and strengthening physical access controls.

Best Practices for Hardware Protection

1. **Enforce hardware hardening:** BIOS passwords, Secure Boot, TPM, encryption.

2. Separate critical systems from general office equipment.

3. Test backup restoration procedures regularly.

4. Track assets and reconcile inventories frequently.

5. Integrate environmental alerts into monitoring dashboards. Environmental monitoring should include temperature, humidity, and water-leak detection in critical rooms. Alerts should be tested during periodic recovery drills.

Exam Tip #62

Know when to apply hardware-specific protections such as port locks, tamper-evident seals, chassis intrusion detection, and full-disk encryption.

Network Forensics and Evidence Handling

When a breach or suspicious activity occurs, the organization must be prepared to investigate quickly and accurately. Network forensics focuses on collecting and analyzing data from logs, network flows, and packet captures to reconstruct events. Proper evidence handling is crucial—not only for internal investigations but also for potential legal proceedings.

Forensic Readiness and Preparation

Preparation significantly increases the quality and usefulness of evidence. Being properly prepared is one of the best mitigation strategies that any organization can enforce.

Establish Policies

Define roles, approved procedures, and limitations for evidence collection. Policies should also define which teams are allowed to handle sensitive data.

Synchronize Time

All network devices must use NTP or another reliable time source. Accurate timestamps allow investigators to correlate events across systems. Time mismatch can cause numerous issues outside of just the security implications. Imagine if you had an invalid timestamp and were trying to audit the chain of events regarding an incident.

Enable Comprehensive Logging

Firewalls, servers, switches, DNS systems, proxies, and authentication services must log detailed events. Logs should be centralized in a SIEM or log management system and protected against tampering.

Prepare Forensic Kits.

Kits should include

1. Write blockers

2. Imaging tools

3. Blank storage media

4. Evidence labels

5. Tamper-evident bags

6. Chain-of-custody forms. Forensic readiness improves when evidence handling is standardized: use chain-of-custody forms, hash critical artifacts (e.g., SHA-256), and store evidence in a controlled, access-logged location.

Train Staff

Incident response teams must know how to acquire evidence without altering it and how to escalate cases to legal counsel or law enforcement when needed. Staff is constantly at the forefront of our environment, whether with human interaction or with system support. As such, they are not only the most critical to keep trained but they are the most likely to directly cause an issue.

Collecting Network Evidence

Different types of evidence support different investigative questions. You need to not only be able to recognize the difference but understand what it maps to and how it is impacting the overall network architecture.

Packet Captures (PCAP)

Tools like Wireshark and tcpdump capture live network traffic. TAPs or SPAN ports provide continuous access to traffic streams. Packet captures provide payload-level detail when legally permissible.

Flow Records

NetFlow, sFlow, and IPFIX provide summaries of traffic patterns without exposing payloads. These records are essential for identifying large file transfers, command-and-control traffic, and exfiltration behavior.

Log Files

Firewall logs, IDS alerts, DHCP logs, DNS queries, and system authentication events provide context. SIEM queries allow investigators to pivot between sources and build timelines.

Endpoint Artifacts

RAM captures, system logs, file metadata, and browser histories can reveal malicious activity. Disk imaging must use write blockers to preserve integrity.

Chain of Custody and Preservation

In the world of forensics, the value of evidence is directly tied to how it is handled from the moment of discovery. To be **admissible** in a court of law or for a formal corporate audit, evidence must be preserved correctly through a rigorous, documented process.

Documentation and Tracking

The **Chain of Custody** is a chronological record of everyone who has had possession of a piece of evidence. Any gap in this record can lead to the evidence being dismissed.

- **Activity Logs:** Record every action taken, including who collected the evidence, the exact time and date, the location, and the conditions under which it was found.

- **Device Identification:** Include serial numbers, hardware IDs, and model numbers for all physical devices collected.

- **Contextual Notes:** Use standardized chain-of-custody forms (such as those following **ISO/IEC 27037** or **SWGDE** guidance) and include the system state, logged-in users, and specific collection methods.

Integrity and Integrity Validation

Proving that the evidence has not been altered is essential for maintaining its "forensic soundness."

- **Write Blocking:** Always use hardware write blockers when imaging drives to prevent the host operating system from accidentally modifying the original data.

- **Hashing for Integrity:** Generate a digital fingerprint, such as an **SHA-256** hash, immediately after collection.

- **Verification Redundancy:** Use both SHA-256 and MD5 hashes (where legally acceptable) for redundancy to ensure the data is immutable.

- **Storage and Handoffs:** Store hashes separately from the evidence and validate them automatically during intake or any analysis workflow to detect any unintended changes.

Evidence Storage and Protection

Physical and digital artifacts must be protected from environmental damage and unauthorized access.

- **Secured Facilities:** Store evidence in a locked evidence cabinet or an isolated forensic analysis lab with restricted access.

- **Access Control:** Utilize multi-factor authentication (MFA), access logging, and audit trails for all evidence storage areas.

- **Environmental Safety:** Use fireproof and tamper-evident cabinets for physical media to protect against disasters and sabotage.

Hashing

Generate SHA-256 or similar hashes for digital evidence. Recalculate hashes after copying to confirm integrity. This ensures the integrity of data throughout the formal process of investigation.

Write Blocking

Hardware write blockers prevent accidental modification during imaging or analysis. This is crucial in any forensic review. Without properly enforcing write blocking, it is very possible to incidentally delete or alter key evidence.

Real-World Example: Tracking Data Exfiltration

A security team notices a spike in outbound traffic. Flow records show large transfers to an unknown IP. Firewall logs reveal encrypted traffic over port 443. Investigators create a packet capture using a SPAN port and, with proper authorization, decrypt the traffic using the server's private key. They discover archives of sensitive documents being uploaded. The server is isolated, forensic images are captured, and a full investigation begins with proper documentation and hash validation.

Best Practices for Forensics and Evidence Handling

1. Automate and centralize log collection.

2. Capture volatile memory before powering down systems.

3. Follow legal, regulatory, and privacy requirements.

4. Use isolated systems for forensic analysis.

5. Conduct post-incident reviews to strengthen processes.

Exam Tip #63

Expect questions about first-priority evidence (volatile data), chain-of-custody steps, hashing, and the difference between packet captures and flow records.

Chapter Summary

Physical security and forensics provide the foundational protection upon which all cybersecurity rests. Layered perimeter defenses, controlled access to buildings and server rooms, and comprehensive surveillance systems create an environment where unauthorized physical access is difficult and quickly detected. Hardware protections, environmental controls, and asset management further safeguard IT infrastructure from tampering, theft, and natural hazards.

When security incidents do occur, forensic readiness ensures that evidence is captured properly and preserved with integrity. Through synchronized timestamps, centralized logging, careful documentation, hashing, write-blocking, and controlled storage, investigators can reconstruct events and support internal or legal actions with confidence.

Mastering these disciplines strengthens your ability to protect infrastructure holistically and positions you for success in environments where physical and digital risks converge. They are core elements of professional network management and are directly tested on the Network+ exam.

CHAPTER 13

Network Management and Documentation

A network that "works" is not the same as a network that is manageable. The difference is process. When performance slips or an outage hits, you don't want to be guessing which switch feeds which closet, who changed a VLAN last week, or whether a WAN circuit has been quietly dropping packets for months.

Network management is the discipline of keeping an environment visible, controlled, and recoverable. That starts with monitoring—collecting performance and availability data so you can detect problems early and respond with evidence instead of assumptions. It continues with configuration management and change control so device settings remain consistent, changes are deliberate, and rollback is possible.

Documentation ties the whole operation together. Accurate diagrams, IP records, config backups, and changing logs reduce downtime, speed onboarding, and make troubleshooting far more efficient. In this chapter, you'll work through the practices that keep networks stable: monitoring and baselining, configuration control, and the documentation habits that support daily operations and compliance.

© Kodi A. Cochran 2026
K. A. Cochran, *CompTIA Network+ (N10-009) Certification Companion,*
Certification Study Companion Series, https://doi.org/10.1007/979-8-8688-2341-1_13

Network Monitoring and Performance Visibility

Network monitoring is the ongoing observation of systems, links, applications, and services to understand how they perform over time. Monitoring helps identify early signs of degradation, detect failures quickly, and measure the impact of changes. Without monitoring data, teams lose visibility and end up relying on user reports, which delays diagnosis and extends outages.

Good monitoring combines real-time visibility, historical trend analysis, and alerting thresholds that fire when conditions move outside normal ranges. The goal isn't to collect data for its own sake, but the goal is to shorten mean time to detect (MTTD) and mean time to resolve (MTTR) by giving you actionable signals.

Key Performance Metrics

Performance metrics are the signals that tell you what the network is doing. One metric rarely tells the whole story, so the real skill is correlation—compare latency, jitter, packet loss, utilization, and error counters together so you can separate congestion from physical layer faults and misconfigurations.

Latency

Latency is the delay between a request and its response, measured in milliseconds. It matters most for interactive traffic such as voice, video, gaming, and remote desktops. Increased latency can indicate congestion, inefficient routing, overloaded devices, or processing delays on a firewall or VPN concentrator. Ping, traceroute, and pathping are commonly used to diagnose latency across network hops and pinpoint where delays begin.

Jitter

Jitter is variation in packet arrival time. Even when average latency looks acceptable, high jitter can ruin quality and video performance because real-time streams depend on consistent timing. Congested links, oversubscribed WAN circuits, and inconsistent queuing behavior are common jitter culprits. QoS is often the practical fix when voice and video must compete with bulk transfers.

Packet Loss

Packet loss is the percentage of packets that never arrive. Persistent loss can point to congestion, overloaded interfaces, damaged cabling, faulty ports, failing transceivers, or wireless interference. Flow monitoring and SNMP counters can help identify links experiencing packet loss, and interface counters help confirm whether the issue is physical or capacity-related.

Bandwidth Utilization

Bandwidth utilization compares current usage to available capacity. Short spikes are normal, but sustained peaks during predictable busy periods usually require action—QoS policies, scheduling non-critical transfers off-peak, circuit upgrades, or redesigning traffic flows. NetFlow, sFlow, or IPFIX data is especially useful for identifying top talkers and confirming what traffic is actually driving utilization.

Error Rates

Error counters—CRC errors, input/output drops, and other interface errors—often point to physical layer issues. If you see increasing CRC or input error counters, start by checking patch cables, connectors, optics, and duplex/speed mismatches. Errors that trend upward over time are a strong indicator that a link is degrading and needs attention before it fails.

Availability and Uptime

Availability measures whether systems and services are reachable. Uptime targets are often expressed as a percentage, and monitoring platforms track outages by alerting when devices stop responding. Common monitoring systems include Nagios, Zabbix, and PRTG for tracking uptime and triggering outage alerts.

Monitoring Tools and Protocols

Monitoring isn't a single tool, it's a toolkit. The best approach uses device telemetry, traffic analytics, and log data together so you can see both symptoms and root causes. Most environments combine NMS, centralized logging, and flow analytics.

SNMP (Simple Network Management Protocol)

SNMP collects performance data from devices: interface statistics, CPU usage, memory usage, and status information. Platforms like SolarWinds, PRTG, Zabbix, and Nagios use SNMP polling for regular metrics and SNMP traps for event-driven alerts. SNMPv3 provides authentication and encryption, unlike earlier versions, and should be used whenever possible.

NetFlow, sFlow, and IPFIX

Flow protocols summarize traffic patterns, identify top talkers, and help administrators understand who is communicating and how much bandwidth they are consuming. They support detailed traffic accounting, bandwidth analysis, and anomaly detection. NetFlow is commonly associated with Cisco, sFlow is widely used in switching environments, and IPFIX is an IETF standard.

Ping and Traceroute

Ping verifies reachability and provides basic latency measurements. Traceroute identifies the path traffic takes and highlights where delays or failures begin. Pathping is also useful in Windows environments because it combines hop discovery with ongoing loss measurement. Keep in mind that ICMP can be filtered or rate-limited, so interpret results in context.

Syslog and Centralized Logging

Syslog servers aggregate event logs from routers, switches, firewalls, and servers. Logs reveal link failures, configuration changes, authentication attempts, and security events—critical evidence during investigations. Secure logging practices include retention policies, access control, and protecting log transport when possible (e.g., TLS-enabled collectors).

Synthetic Monitoring and Application Tests

Synthetic monitoring tests application workflows (HTTP, DNS, email, VoIP, and other service checks) to expose user-visible problems that device metrics may miss. The strongest monitoring posture correlates SNMP metrics, flow analytics, syslog events, and synthetic tests for a full-stack view of network health.

Establishing Baselines

A performance baseline represents normal operating conditions across specific time periods. Baselines are essential because they let you differentiate normal fluctuations from emerging problems. Defining normal ranges and threshold values for latency, jitter, error rates, retransmissions, and interface resets makes alerting meaningful and reduces false positives.

Baselines typically include

1. Normal latency ranges

2. Typical bandwidth usage patterns

3. Expected error rate thresholds

4. Usual CPU and memory utilization

5. Traffic patterns at peak and off-peak hours

Baselines should be updated periodically to reflect changes in applications or network architecture. When problems occur, compare current metrics to baseline behavior before making changes.

Real-World Example: Intermittent VoIP Complaints

Users report call issues in the early afternoon. Monitoring reveals increased jitter and packet loss on a key WAN link during peak hours. Using flow analytics, administrators identify non-critical file transfers consuming excessive bandwidth. QoS is applied to prioritize voice traffic, and bulk transfers are scheduled off-peak, resolving the problem.

Monitoring Best Practices

Monitoring is only useful if it drives action. The goal is consistent visibility, clear thresholds, and enough historical data to explain what changed.

1. Establish and regularly update performance baselines.

2. Set thresholds and automated alerts for key metrics.

3. Use both real-time and historical analysis to identify trends.

4. Monitor from multiple vantage points (internal, cloud, remote sites).

5. Correlate SNMP, flow analytics, syslog, and synthetic tests when troubleshooting.

Exam Tip #64

Know the key performance metrics (latency, jitter, packet loss) and the tools used to monitor them. Expect questions asking you to interpret symptoms based on metric deviations.

Configuration Management and Change Control

While monitoring provides real-time visibility, configuration management keeps the environment stable over the long term. Configuration management involves documenting, saving, and validating device settings. Change control ensures updates are evaluated and deployed without disrupting operations.

Configuration Management Elements

Configuration management is about consistency and recoverability. If a device fails or a change introduces problems, you should be able to restore well-good configuration quickly.

Configuration Backups

Maintain versioned backups of router, switch, firewall, and server configurations. Label backups with timestamps, device IDs, and version numbers, and store them securely. If backups contain sensitive information, encrypt them at rest and restrict access.

Configuration Baselines

Baselines establish standard configurations for devices and platforms. Configuration drift is deviation from an approved baseline due to unauthorized changes, ad hoc troubleshooting edits, or sprawl. Baselines make drift easy to detect and correct.

Automation and Configuration Management Tools

Automation improves scalability, repeatability, and rollbacks. Tools like Ansible, RANCID, Cisco Prime, Terraform, and Puppet can automate deployment and tracking, reduce human error, and make changes reviewable.

Configuration Audits

Regular audits compare current settings to baselines and identify unauthorized or unintended changes. Audits can reveal exposed management interfaces, unencrypted services, weak authentication settings, and other non-compliant configurations.

Change-Control Process

A change-control process should define the purpose of the change, affected systems, timeline, impact assessment, and business justification. Changes should be approved by designated approvers (system owners, department leaders, or a Change Advisory Board). Every planned change should include rollback plans for stability or performance issues post-deployment, and outcomes should be documented for future reference.

Real-World Example: Undocumented VLAN Misconfiguration

A network engineer modifies a switch configuration without documenting the change. Days later, connectivity issues arise due to an undocumented VLAN misassignment. A configuration audit reveals the deviation, and the switch is rolled back to the last known-good configuration. After the incident, the organization formalizes mandatory change requests with impact analysis, rollback testing, and approval before live deployment.

Best Practices for Configuration and Change Management

1. Enforcing change control and disciplined configuration management prevents avoidable outages and makes troubleshooting faster.

2. Enforce change control policies across all IT teams.

3. Automate configuration backups and compare versions.

4. Maintain a centralized configuration repository.

5. Schedule regular audits and peer reviews of changes.

6. Document outcomes, approvals, and rollback steps for each change.

Exam Tip #65

Be prepared to identify the role of configuration backups, documentation, and rollback procedures in a stable network. Expect questions on detecting configuration drift and restoring baselines.

Network Documentation and Operational Records

Proactive management must be backed by thorough documentation. Documentation enables consistent support, troubleshooting, expansion, and auditing. Without accurate, up-to-date records, organizations risk drift, longer outages, and failed compliance audits.

Types of Network Documentation

Comprehensive network documentation must capture both logical and physical views of the environment, alongside the operational history that explains how the network has evolved over time. This documentation reduces downtime, accelerates the onboarding of new staff, and significantly increases troubleshooting efficiency.

Physical and Logical Topology Diagrams

Visual representations are essential for understanding the network layout.

- **Physical Network Diagrams**: These illustrate the actual physical layout, including device locations, cabling paths, patch panels, racks, and wiring closets. They help technicians quickly locate hardware during outages or maintenance.

- **Logical Network Diagrams**: These represent the logical structure, such as IP address schemes, subnets, VLAN assignments, and routing relationships. They are vital for planning network segmentation and auditing design against security policies.

Configuration Files and Baselines

These function as repositories of saved configuration states that serve as critical references for recovery, auditing, and compliance.

- **Configuration Documentation**: Includes saved configuration files for routers, switches, firewalls, and wireless controllers.

- **Version Control**: Documentation should record firmware versions, authentication methods, and NAT policies to enable a rollback to known-good states after a failure.

- **Baselines**: These establish a reference point for normal network performance, allowing administrators to differentiate between normal fluctuations and emerging problems.

IP Address Management (IPAM)

IPAM involves maintaining records of IP allocations, subnet usage, and reserved addresses to support DHCP planning and DNS integration.

- **Tracking**: It tracks the usage of IP addresses across the organization, including subnet maps and static address assignments.

- **Conflict Prevention**: Proper IPAM prevents address conflicts, ensures availability, and aids in future network expansion or redesign.

Rack and Floor Diagrams

These provide the physical layouts of equipment in data centers and telecom rooms to support ongoing maintenance and expansion.

- **Equipment Cataloging**: Diagrams should identify the specific location of every switch, server, and UPS within a rack.

- **Inventory Lists**: These complement diagrams by cataloging serial numbers, device models, and warranty periods to streamline procurement and maintenance schedules.

Change Logs

Change logs provide historical records of modifications, detailing who made the change, when it occurred, and the business justification.

- **Accountability**: They support accountability by ensuring every modification is reviewed and approved.

- **Rollback Support**: Historical records allow for faster rollback decisions if a recent change causes unforeseen performance issues or outages.

Access Control and Credential Records

These records document administrative access methods, authentication requirements, and account ownership for audits and security reviews.

- **Security Best Practices**: Sensitive credentials and SNMP community strings should never be stored in plaintext inside diagrams; they should be referenced through a secure password manager or vault.

- **Audit Readiness**: Maintaining clear records of who has administrative access and the specific authentication methods required (such as MFA) is essential for passing compliance audits.

Documentation Tools

Use tools that match your organization's workflow, then standardize templates and storage so documentation stays usable over time.

1. Microsoft Visio, draw.io, and Lucidchart for diagrams

2. Wiki platforms or ITSM systems (e.g., ServiceNow) for operational records

3. IPAM solutions such as phpIPAM or Infoblox

Documentation Best Practices

Documentation should be centralized, version-controlled when possible, and updated immediately after changes. Standard templates and clear labeling make documentation easier to maintain and easier for new staff to use.

1. Centralize documentation and keep it version-controlled.

2. Update records immediately after any network change.

3. Use diagrams and plain language to improve readability.

4. Conduct periodic audits to verify accuracy and completeness.

Exam Tip #66

Be prepared to answer questions on types of network documentation and how they support maintenance, troubleshooting, audits, and regulatory compliance.

Chapter Summary

In this chapter, you developed a working understanding of the practices that support network stability, visibility, and growth. You reviewed key monitoring metrics such as latency, jitter, packet loss, utilization, and error rates, along with the tools used to track them. You then explored configuration management and structured change control, including backups, baselines, audits, and rollback procedures. Finally, you examined the documentation that supports troubleshooting, compliance, and long-term planning.

Mastering these disciplines helps you reduce downtime, respond faster to incidents, and maintain predictable operations. They also represent core Network+ exam themes, especially in scenario-based questions.

CHAPTER 14

Network Policies, Procedures, and Compliance

Technical controls matter, but policies and procedures decide whether those controls are applied consistently. In real environments, most security failures don't start with a "mystery exploit"—they start with weak process: users who never signed an acceptable use policy, accounts that weren't disabled on exit, devices that weren't patched, and logs that weren't retained long enough to reconstruct what happened.

This chapter focuses on the administrative layer of security: acceptable use policies, user life cycle procedures, compliance requirements, and the security frameworks used to structure controls and prepare for audits. These topics show up on the Network+ exam because they reflect how organizations actually run networks on a scale.

Acceptable Use and Core Security Policies

Acceptable Use Policies (AUPs) define what users and third parties are allowed to do with an organization's systems and network resources. AUPs set expectations up front, reduce legal and operational risk, and provide a defensible baseline when violations occur.

© Kodi A. Cochran 2026
K. A. Cochran, *CompTIA Network+ (N10-009) Certification Companion*,
Certification Study Companion Series, https://doi.org/10.1007/979-8-8688-2341-1_14

An AUP is only useful if it stays current. Policies should be reviewed on a schedule (at least annually) and also when the organization changes tools, workflows, or risk posture. If users change roles or projects, scope updates otherwise access and behavior expectations drift out of alignment.

Components of an Acceptable Use Policy

A strong AUP is specific enough to guide behavior without becoming unreadable. It should clearly communicate what is allowed, what is prohibited, and how enforcement works.

Scope of Access

Defines what systems, services, and data a user is permitted to access. Access should align with job requirements, and users should be explicitly prohibited from accessing systems or data outside that scope. These should always follow role based and integrate the principle of least privilege.

Prohibited Activities

Blocks unauthorized use such as installing unapproved software, attempting to bypass security controls, accessing illegal or offensive content, or using corporate systems for personal business.

Device and Resource Use

Specifies rules for company-owned devices, personal devices (BYOD), removable media, internet access, and approved applications. There are various different policies in regard to resource and device usage and it is always best to follow the governing organization and their pre-approved policies.

Monitoring and Enforcement

Notifies users that activity may be logged, monitored, and audited. Defines consequences for violations and escalation paths to HR, legal, or leadership as required.

Acknowledgment and Training

Requires signed acknowledgment and training so users understand the policy. Retraining should occur annually and after major security incidents or material policy changes. This ensures that employees are not only completing training but acknowledging completion and success of the course.

Common Security Policy Types

Security policies define how controls are applied to protect assets. They usually complement the AUP by describing technical requirements—password standards, account lockout rules, access controls, and device configuration expectations.

Administrative and Technical Security Policies

The following policies define the administrative and technical safeguards required to protect organizational assets and maintain compliance within a modern network environment.

Password Policies

These policies establish requirements for "memorized secrets" to prevent unauthorized access. Current industry standards, such as **NIST SP 800-63B**, emphasize length and real-world security over complex character patterns.

- **Minimum Requirements**: Define a minimum length (NIST suggests **8 characters**, though many organizations mandate **12–15+**) and allow all printable ASCII and Unicode characters, including spaces.

- **Modern Approaches**: Shift toward **passphrases** to improve memorability and strength, and avoid mandatory complexity rules (e.g., forced special characters) that can frustrate users and lead to weaker choices.

- **Life Cycle Management**: Discourage periodic password rotation unless there is evidence of compromise.

- **Advanced Authentication**: Many organizations are moving toward **password less** approaches using biometrics and hardware tokens (FIDO2) to improve usability and significantly reduce phishing risk.

Account Lockout Policies

These policies are designed to thwart automated **brute-force** or dictionary attacks by disabling an account after consecutive failed attempts.

- **Thresholds**: Define a reasonable number of consecutive failed login attempts (e.g., **3 to 10**) within a specific time window.

- **Duration**: Specify a lockout duration (e.g., **15–30 minutes**) or require administrative intervention to unlock the account.

- **Risk Note**: Be aware that overly aggressive lockout policies can be used as a **Denial of Service (DoS)** vector, where an attacker intentionally locks out legitimate users.

Access Control Policies

Access control ensures that users and systems are only granted the permissions necessary to perform their roles, following the **Principle of Least Privilege (PoLP)**.

- **Privileged Accounts**: Define strict handling for administrative accounts, requiring **Multi-Factor Authentication (MFA)** and **just-in-time (JIT)** elevation.

- **Reviews and Audits**: Conduct periodic access reviews (e.g., quarterly) to identify "**privilege creep**," where users accumulate permissions they no longer need.

- **Traceability**: Ensure all access and administrative actions generate **audit trails** (logs) to provide oversight and accountability.

Device Security Policies

These policies govern the security posture of both corporate-owned and **Bring Your Own Device (BYOD)** endpoints.

- **Endpoint Protection**: Mandate antivirus or Endpoint Detection and Response (EDR) software to monitor for and block malware.

- **Hardening**: Define configuration expectations, such as disabling unused ports/services, removing default credentials, and enforcing **BIOS/UEFI passwords**.

- **Patch Management**: Require timely installation of operating system and firmware patches to mitigate known vulnerabilities (CVEs).

- **Compliance**: For BYOD, utilize **Mobile Device Management (MDM)** to enforce the separation of personal and corporate data and enable remote wipe capabilities for lost devices.

Data Classification Policies

Data classification provides a framework for identifying the sensitivity of information and determining appropriate handling controls.

- **Classification Tiers**: Common levels include

- **Public**: Information that can be shared freely without risk.

- **Internal**: Operational details that should stay within the organization but carry low risk.

- **Confidential**: Sensitive information (e.g., employee records) requiring access restrictions.

- **Restricted/Top Secret**: Highly sensitive data (e.g., strategic plans) requiring the highest level of encryption and auditing.

- **Handling Controls**: For each tier, define required controls such as **encryption** (at rest and in transit), specific access restrictions, and defined **retention rules** for storage and disposal.

Real-World Example: Malware from Unapproved Software

A mid-sized organization experiences a malware outbreak traced back to an employee downloading unapproved software. The incident review shows the AUP was outdated, enforcement was inconsistent, and users were unaware of the risks. The organization updates the AUP to explicitly prohibit unapproved installations, tightens web filtering, and implements mandatory annual awareness training. They also formalize escalation procedures for violations so response is consistent.

Best Practices for Policy Management

Policies should be made so they can be enforced. The best policies are reviewed, owned, distributed, acknowledged, and audited—otherwise they become shelfware.

1. Align policies with recognized standards (NIST, ISO/IEC 27001, CIS Controls) to ensure coverage.

2. Involve HR, legal, and IT stakeholders during creation and revision.

3. Assign ownership of each policy to a role or department for accountability.

4. Track policy acceptance electronically so acknowledgments are auditable.

5. Review policies on schedule and after major incidents or operational changes.

Exam Tip #67

Be familiar with AUP components, common security policy types, and how enforcement reduces security risk. Expect scenario-based questions about policy violations and appropriate responses.

Onboarding, Offboarding, and Role-Based Access Control

User life cycle management is security control. The moment an account is created, it becomes part of your attack surface. The moment an account should be removed, it becomes a risk if it lingers. Onboarding and offboarding procedures exist to keep access aligned with employment status and job function.

Onboarding Procedures

Onboarding should be checklist-driven so steps are completed consistently. Account provisioning should be role-based, documented, and auditable. Integrating automated provisioning with HR systems improves accuracy and creates a reliable audit trail for who approved what access and when.

1. Account provisioning based on job role using directory services (e.g., Active Directory)

2. Permission assignment using least privilege and standardized role templates

3. Orientation and security awareness training, including AUP acknowledgment

4. Device assignment, asset tagging, and inventory logging

Offboarding Procedures

Offboarding must be fast and complete. The most common failure is partial offboarding—one account is disabled but a VPN token is still active, a shared drive link remains, or a privileged group membership was never removed. Centralizing offboarding checklists and logging actions in a compliance-tracking platform or SIEM improves accountability.

1. **Immediate access revocation:** Disable accounts, VPN access, email, and MFA tokens.

2. Return and recovery of company-owned assets (laptops, badges, tokens, mobile devices).

3. Removal from distribution lists, privileged groups, and shared resource access.

4. Documentation of offboarding steps for audit and investigation purposes.

5. For high-value assets or devices containing sensitive data, chain-of-custody forms can help document possession and reduce disputes during investigations.

Role-Based Access Control (RBAC)

RBAC assigns permissions based on roles instead of individual-by-individual access decisions. Users are placed into roles (such as HR, Accounting, IT Support) with predefined access profiles. This improves consistency, reduces over-privilege, and makes onboarding/offboarding faster and less error-prone.

RBAC is most effective when roles reflect job functions rather than departments. If roles are too broad, users inherit access they don't need. Periodic access reviews, especially for privileged accounts, help detect stale group memberships, shadow IT access paths, and legacy permissions.

Best Practices for User Life Cycle Management

User life cycle security depends on speed, consistency, and verification. The goal is to prevent lingering access paths while keeping onboarding efficient.

1. Automate provisioning and deprovisioning where possible using identity life cycle tools.

2. Perform access audits to detect lingering access paths (shared drives, stale groups, shadow IT).

3. Conduct periodic privileged access reviews (PAR) and consider just-in-time access for admin roles.

4. Integrate offboarding with asset recovery and credential revocation.

5. Use logging and asset tracking to support audits and digital forensics.

Exam Tip #68

Expect questions involving account provisioning, termination, and role-based access management. Be able to identify risks in inconsistent offboarding or improper RBAC assignment.

Compliance Standards and Legal Regulations

Compliance is the intersection of technical controls, documented process, and legal obligation. Regulations vary by industry and geography, but the pattern is consistent: organizations must protect sensitive data, control access, retain evidence, and report incidents appropriately.

GDPR (General Data Protection Regulation)

Governs the handling of personal data for EU residents. It requires lawful processing, data minimization, breach notification, and grants rights such as deletion. Penalties can be significant (commonly cited as up to €20 million or 4% of global annual revenue, whichever is higher).

HIPAA (Health Insurance Portability and Accountability Act)

Regulates protected health information (PHI) in the United States. It requires administrative, physical, and technical safeguards, including access controls and audit controls. Covered entities and business associates typically formalize responsibilities through agreements and documented procedures.

SOX (Sarbanes-Oxley Act)

Applies to public companies in the United States. It requires accurate financial reporting and verifiable internal controls. From a technical standpoint, this often translates to strict access control, change-management logging, and retention of relevant system records.

PCI DSS (Payment Card Industry Data Security Standard)

Applies to any organization that stores, processes, or transmits cardholder data. It requires strong access controls, secure transmission, segmentation, and continuous monitoring of systems in scope.

IT Compliance Practices

Compliance work is mostly operational. It requires policies that map to legal requirements, controls that are implemented consistently, and documentation that proves those controls are working.

1. **Data handling policies**: Retention, encryption, and access requirements based on classification.

2. **Security framework adoption**: Mapping controls to NIST CSF, ISO/IEC 27001, or CIS Controls.

3. **Audit trail protection**: Centralized logs that are secured and tamper-evident.

4. **Compliance training**: Staff education on required behaviors and reporting responsibilities.

Best Practices for Compliance

Most compliance failures are process failures: missing documentation, untrained staff, and controls that were never verified. Continuous review keeps the organization out of "audit panic mode."

1. Stay updated on regulatory changes and refresh policies accordingly.

2. Map internal policies and technical controls directly to compliance requirements.

3. Use GRC tools or structured tracking to manage obligations and evidence.

4. Conduct internal audits and third-party assessments on schedule.

5. Reinforce training annually and after major incidents or policy changes.

Exam Tip #69

Be prepared to identify the purpose and high-level requirements of GDPR, HIPAA, SOX, and PCI DSS. Know how documentation, access control, logging, and encryption support compliance.

Security Frameworks and Audit Readiness

Frameworks provide structure. Instead of inventing policy and control coverage from scratch, organizations use security frameworks to ensure their controls are comprehensive, consistent, and aligned with business and regulatory goals.

NIST Cybersecurity Framework (CSF)

Organizes security into Identify, Protect, Detect, Respond, and Recover. It also supports profiles and maturity discussions so organizations can prioritize improvements.

ISO/IEC 27001

An international standard for information security management systems (ISMS). It emphasizes risk management, documentation, and demonstrating control effectiveness.

CIS Controls

A prioritized set of defensive actions grouped into implementation tiers to help organizations adopt controls based on available resources.

COBIT

An IT governance framework that aligns security, privacy, and governance objectives to business strategy and accountability.

Audit Preparation Steps

Audit readiness is about evidence. Auditors want to see policy documentation, proof that controls were implemented, proof that controls were reviewed, and proof that issues were corrected.

1. Define audit scope and boundaries (in-scope assets, stakeholders, required artifacts).

2. Review policies, configuration baselines, and logs for completeness and accuracy.

3. Perform internal assessments or mock audits to find gaps early.

4. Remediate issues and document corrective actions taken.

5. Store audit artifacts in secure, version-controlled repositories (SharePoint, GRC tools, controlled repositories).

Continuous monitoring and baseline enforcement help maintain compliance between audits. SIEM tools are commonly used for centralized logging and evidence collection.

Real-World Example: PCI DSS Audit Preparation

A retail organization preparing for a PCI DSS audit uses CIS Controls as a guide for internal review. The team discovered that employee access to payment systems was not consistently logged. They correct the logging configuration, update procedures, and validate evidence collection before the formal audit—allowing them to pass without critical findings.

Best Practices for Frameworks and Audits

Framework adoption should not be a one-time project. The strongest programs build continuous review into operations and treat audits as verification, not a scramble.

1. Choose a framework that fits your industry and organizational maturity.

2. Keep audit-related documentation organized, current, and version-controlled.

3. Protect log integrity with centralized collection and restricted access.

4. Integrate framework assessments into ongoing risk management cycles.

5. Use third-party assessments for unbiased validation when appropriate.

Exam Tip #70

Expect questions on common security frameworks and how they support policy enforcement and compliance. Understand how audit readiness relies on documentation, logging, and procedural consistency.

Chapter Summary

This chapter covers the administrative and compliance-driven controls that govern secure network operations. You reviewed acceptable use policies and core security policies, along with practical enforcement and training considerations. You examined onboarding and offboarding procedures, including role-based access control as a scalable way to manage permissions. You also covered major compliance drivers and the security frameworks organizations used to structure controls and prepare for audits.

These topics reinforce an important reality: technical security is only as strong as the processes that apply it. Strong policy, consistent procedures, and defensible documentation are what make security repeatable and auditable.

CHAPTER 15

Exam Preparation and Strategy

The CompTIA Network+ (N10-009) exam is structured around five primary domains. Mastery of these domains ensures comprehensive understanding of networking principles and prepares you for a variety of real-world scenarios you may encounter in professional environments. Emphasize that mastering all exam domains prepares candidates for real-world networking scenarios.

Network+ Exam Domains

1. **Networking Fundamentals (24%)** Recognize that Networking Fundamentals and Troubleshooting domains carry greater weight; allocate study time accordingly.

   - OSI and TCP/IP models

   - Common networking protocols and ports

   - Wireless standards and technologies

   - Network topologies and types

K. A. Cochran, *CompTIA Network+ (N10-009) Certification Companion,*
Certification Study Companion Series, https://doi.org/10.1007/979-8-8688-2341-1_15

2. **Network Implementations (19%)**

- Deploying routers, switches, access points, and firewalls. Browser-based simulators to practice CLI commands for switches and routers (show, ping, tracert, ipconfig, etc.).

- Configuring IPv4/IPv6

- VLANs, trunking, and inter-VLAN routing

- WAN and remote access technologies

3. **Network Operations (16%)**

- Performance monitoring and optimization

- Configuration management and documentation

- Disaster recovery and high availability

- Policies and procedures

4. **Network Security (19%)**

- Physical and logical security devices

- Authentication and access control

- Common attacks and mitigation strategies

- Secure network design and remote access

5. **Network Troubleshooting (22%)**

- Troubleshooting methodologies

- Diagnosing hardware, software, and cable issues

- Packet capture and log analysis

- Common wireless and connectivity problems

Stay abreast of evolving trends such as SD-WAN, cloud-native networking, and automation tools, which extend beyond Network+ but reflect real-world expectations.

Tips for Domain Review

1. Create flashcards or quick-reference sheets per domain.

2. Focus extra time on your weakest domain(s) using practice exams.

3. Revisit hands-on labs to reinforce technical tasks.

4. Tie topics to real-world examples to improve retention.

Approach PBQs with process-of-elimination, careful review of configuration syntax, and attention to context (e.g., IP schemes, interface labels).

Exam Tip #71

Be familiar with the percentage weighting of each domain. Expect a heavier concentration of questions from Networking Fundamentals and Troubleshooting.

The official exam blueprint as a checklist and map each objective to personal notes and lab exercises.

Introduction to Exam Readiness

As you approach the final phase of your Network+ certification journey, it's critical to reinforce your understanding, refine your problem-solving skills, and develop a sound strategy for exam day. This chapter provides a structured framework for reviewing the exam domains, interpreting question types, and applying effective test-taking techniques.

Whether you're reviewing under pressure or pacing your study across weeks, this chapter will guide you through actionable tactics that align with the structure and expectations of the CompTIA Network+ exam. Use the exam timer strategically to pace yourself across 15–20-question segments. Some questions test concept familiarity more than configuration; answer these quickly if sure.

Question Types and Test-Taking Strategies

The CompTIA Network+ exam contains a mix of multiple-choice and performance-based questions (PBQs). Understanding the format and practicing strategies can significantly improve your performance. The exam consists of multiple-choice and performance-based questions, both conceptual understanding and practical skills matter.

Question Types:

1. **Multiple-Choice (Single and Multiple Answer):**

   - Most common question type. Read all options carefully before selecting your answer.

2. **Performance-Based Questions (PBQs):** Warn that performance-based questions (PBQs) can be time-consuming; advise flagging them to return later unless confident. Adopt strategies like answering known questions first, flagging complex PBQs, and using elimination to manage pacing and reduce cognitive load.

   - Simulated tasks requiring you to configure settings, troubleshoot scenarios, or drag-and-drop elements.

   - Time-consuming—tackle these after answering all simpler questions unless confident.

3. **Scenario-Based Questions:**

- Present a real-world network issue. Test your ability to analyze symptoms and apply solutions.

4. **Drag-and-Drop Matching:**

- Map terms to definitions, or steps to procedures.

Test-Taking Strategies:

1. **Answer What You Know First:**

- Don't get stuck on one question. Mark, tough ones for review.

2. **Use Process of Elimination:**

- Rule out clearly incorrect answers to improve odds of a correct guess. Policies and procedures should be reviewed regularly; mock exams thoroughly, focusing on the reasoning behind correct and incorrect answers to close knowledge gaps.

3. **Watch the Clock:**

- Budget time—90 questions in 90 minutes means about one minute per question.

4. **Stay Calm During PBQs:**

- Use diagrams, notes, or clues in the question to navigate PBQs logically.

5. **Don't Overthink Easy Questions:**

- The exam includes some straightforward ones— trust your first instinct if you know the concept.

Real-World Strategy Example

A test taker began the exam by skimming through and answering all the multiple-choice questions first, then circled back to the performance-based items. By managing their time wisely, they avoided getting bogged down early and finished with time to review flagged questions.

Practice building and rebuilding networks with different IP schemes and troubleshoot using tools like netstat, arp, and nslookup.

Exam Tip #72

Understand each question format. During the exam, keep track of time and don't let PBQs derail your pacing.

Practice and Study Resources

Preparation goes beyond memorization requires a hands-on understanding of tools, protocols, and troubleshooting methods. Leveraging a mix of study resources reinforces knowledge and builds exam confidence.

Recommended Study Tools:

1. **Official CompTIA Network+ Study Guide:**

   - Comprehensive coverage of all exam objectives with review questions.

2. **CompTIA CertMaster Learn and Labs:**

   - Interactive lessons and performance-based simulations.

3. **Third-Party Video Courses (e.g., Udemy, LinkedIn Learning):**

   - Visual learning for key topics and demonstrations.

4. **Flashcards and Apps:**

   - Tools like Quizlet help reinforce definitions, ports,
     and protocol functions.

5. **Practice Exams:**

   - Simulate real exam conditions. Focus on timing
     and remediation.

Hands-On Practice

1. **Network Simulators:**

   - Emulate switch/router environments (Cisco Packet
     Tracer, GNS3, or Boson NetSim).

2. **Home Lab Setups:**

   - Practice device configuration using physical or
     virtual machines.

3. **Troubleshooting Challenges:**

   - Re-create networking issues and attempt to
     resolve them using logs, pings, traceroutes, and
     config audits.

Real-World Study Approach

One candidate used a combination of video instruction, flashcards, and
daily lab simulations. They created a physical home network using spare
switches and a firewall VM, practicing VLANs, NAT, and DHCP in real time.
This combination led to deeper retention and successful certification.

Best Practices

1. Study in blocks with periodic review sessions.

2. Reinforce learning with active recall and spaced repetition.

3. Don't neglect practical tools and command-line familiarity.

Exam Tip #73

Use a blend of study resources. Focus on real-world tasks, not just memorization. Build confidence with mock exams and practice labs.

Chapter Summary

In this final chapter, you learned how to transition from studying to test readiness by structuring your review process around the official CompTIA Network+ domains. Understanding the weighted focus on fundamentals and troubleshooting ensures smarter time allocation during review sessions.

You examined common question formats, including multiple-choice, PBQs, and scenario-based items, and were given strategies to approach each type with confidence. Techniques like process of elimination, flagging difficult questions, and managing performance-based items effectively can prevent time mismanagement and test fatigue.

Preparation also included curating the best study resources—ranging from official guides and video instruction to flashcards and simulated labs. The value of hands-on practice cannot be overstated, especially in a practical certification like Network+. Network simulators, home labs, and troubleshooting scenarios provide crucial reinforcement.

By applying the strategies outlined in this chapter, you not only boost your exam confidence but also deepen your readiness for real-world networking roles. Remember, certification validates your knowledge, but true expertise is forged through consistent application and continued learning.

Network+ Terms

1. **3-Tier Architecture:** A network design that segments core, distribution, and access layers.

2. **802.1X:** A port-based network access control (NAC) protocol used for authentication.

3. **AAA (Authentication, Authorization, and Accounting):** A framework used to control access and track user activity on networked systems.

4. **ACL (Access Control List):** A set of rules used to control network traffic and reduce network attacks.

5. **Access Control:** Mechanisms that restrict access to systems and data based on defined rules.

6. **Active Directory (AD):** Microsoft's directory service used for user and resource management.

7. **Ad Hoc Network:** A decentralized wireless network formed directly between devices.

8. **Address Resolution Protocol (ARP):** Resolves IP addresses to MAC addresses on a local network.

9. **Anycast:** A network addressing method in which one IP address routes to the nearest of multiple servers.

10. **Application Layer:** The top layer of the OSI model that interfaces with user-facing software.

© Kodi A. Cochran 2026
K. A. Cochran, *CompTIA Network+ (N10-009) Certification Companion,*
Certification Study Companion Series, https://doi.org/10.1007/979-8-8688-2341-1

11. **Backbone:** The central conduit designed to carry the majority of network traffic.

12. **Bandwidth:** The maximum data transfer rate of a network or Internet connection.

13. **Baseline:** A reference point for normal network performance used for comparison.

14. **Beacon Frame:** A wireless management frame used by access points to advertise their presence.

15. **BGP (Border Gateway Protocol):** A routing protocol used to exchange routing information across the Internet.

16. **Bitrate:** The amount of data transmitted over a given time interval, usually measured in bits per second.

17. **Bluejacking:** The sending of unsolicited messages over Bluetooth.

18. **Broadcast Domain:** A logical division where broadcast packets are sent to all devices.

19. **Broadcast Storm:** An excessive amount of broadcast traffic that can congest a network.

20. **Cable Certifier:** A tool used to verify whether a cable meets performance specifications.

21. **Carrier Ethernet:** High-speed Ethernet provided by a telecom carrier for WAN services.

22. **Change Management:** The structured process for approving and documenting network changes.

23. **CIDR (Classless Inter-Domain Routing):** A method for allocating IP addresses and routing.

24. **Collision Domain:** A segment of a network where data packets can collide with one another.

25. **Content Filter:** A device or software that blocks inappropriate or malicious web content.

26. **Crosstalk:** Electromagnetic interference from adjacent cables.

27. **CSMA/CD (Carrier Sense Multiple Access/ Collision Detection):** Protocol for detecting collisions in Ethernet.

28. **Default Gateway:** A router IP address that serves as an access point to external networks.

29. **Demarcation Point (Demarc):** The point where a service provider's responsibility ends and the customer's begins.

30. **DHCP (Dynamic Host Configuration Protocol):** Assigns IP addresses to devices automatically.

31. **Differential Backup:** Backs up all data changed since the last full backup.

32. **DNS (Domain Name System):** Translates domain names to IP addresses.

33. **DMZ (Demilitarized Zone):** A separate network zone that adds a buffer between internal systems and external traffic.

34. **Duplex Mismatch:** A configuration issue where one device is set to full-duplex and the other to half-duplex.

35. **EAP (Extensible Authentication Protocol):** Framework supporting multiple authentication methods.

36. **Egress Traffic:** Data that exits a network to an external destination.

37. **Encapsulation:** The process of enclosing data within another set of data in the network stack.

38. **Firewall:** A device or software that filters traffic based on security rules.

39. **Flood Guard:** A security control designed to prevent DoS/DDoS or MAC flooding attacks.

40. **FQDN (Fully Qualified Domain Name):** A complete domain name that specifies its exact location in the DNS hierarchy.

41. **FTP (File Transfer Protocol):** A protocol used to transfer files between systems over a network.

42. **Gateway:** A device that connects different network architectures.

43. **Geofencing:** Using GPS or RFID to define virtual boundaries that trigger actions.

44. **Hashing:** Converts input data into a fixed-length string for integrity verification.

45. **Honeypot:** A decoy system designed to lure attackers and detect malicious activity.

46. **Hop:** Each point a data packet passes through in a network.

47. **IP Address:** A unique identifier assigned to each device on a network.

48. **IPSec (Internet Protocol Security):** Protocol suite for securing IP communications.

49. **ISP (Internet Service Provider):** A company providing access to the Internet.

50. **Impedance:** Resistance in cabling that affects signal integrity.

51. **Ingress Traffic:** Data that enters a network from an external source.

52. **Jumbo Frames:** Ethernet frames with more than 1500 bytes of payload to improve efficiency.

53. **Kerberos:** A secure authentication protocol using tickets within a trusted third-party system.

54. **LAN (Local Area Network):** A network that connects devices in a limited area like an office.

55. **Latency:** The delay before a transfer of data begins following an instruction.

56. **Load Balancer:** A device or software that distributes network traffic across multiple servers.

57. **Logical Topology:** The arrangement of devices and how they communicate over a network, independent of physical layout.

58. **Loopback Address:** An IP address (typically 127.0.0.1) used to test internal TCP/IP functionality.

59. **MAC Address:** A hardware address that uniquely identifies a device on a network.

60. **Man-in-the-Middle Attack:** An attack where a third party intercepts and possibly alters communications.

61. **MTU (Maximum Transmission Unit):** The size of the largest packet that can be transmitted on a network segment.

62. **Multicast:** Network transmission to a specific group of hosts.

63. **NAC (Network Access Control):** Controls device access based on health and policy compliance.

64. **NAT (Network Address Translation):** Modifies IP address information in packet headers to allow internal systems to share one IP.

65. **Network Tap:** A hardware device that monitors network traffic by duplicating signals.

66. **Nmap:** A network scanning tool used to discover devices and services.

67. **OSI Model:** A conceptual framework that defines how data is transmitted over a network.

68. **Packet:** A unit of data transmitted over a network.

69. **Patch Panel:** A hardware assembly that contains ports used to connect and manage incoming/ outgoing LAN cables.

70. **PBQ (Performance-Based Question):** Practical question type on CompTIA exams requiring interaction.

71. **Ping:** A network tool used to test connectivity.

72. **PoE (Power over Ethernet):** Technology that delivers power and data over Ethernet cables.

73. **Port:** A logical access channel used by applications to communicate.

74. **Protocol:** A set of rules that allow devices to communicate over a network.

75. **Proxy Server:** An intermediary server that separates end users from the websites they browse.

76. **QoS (Quality of Service):** Prioritization of specific types of network traffic.

77. **RAID (Redundant Array of Independent Disks):** A data storage virtualization method for redundancy or performance.

78. **RADIUS (Remote Authentication Dial-In User Service):** Protocol for centralized authentication.

79. **RDP (Remote Desktop Protocol):** Allows remote access to another computer.

80. **Roll-over Cable:** A type of serial cable used to connect a computer terminal to a router's console port.

81. **Router:** A device that forwards data packets between networks.

82. **SAN (Storage Area Network):** A high-speed network that provides access to consolidated storage.

83. **SFP (Small Form-factor Pluggable):** A transceiver used in networking equipment for modular connectivity.

84. **SLA (Service-Level Agreement):** A formal agreement that defines service expectations and responsibilities.

85. **SNMP (Simple Network Management Protocol):** Used to monitor and manage networked devices.

86. **SSID (Service Set Identifier):** The name assigned to a wireless network.

87. **Spanning Tree Protocol (STP):** Prevents switching loops in a bridged network.

88. **Sticky MAC:** A switch port security feature that dynamically learns MAC addresses and restricts access to those addresses.

89. **Subnet:** A segmented piece of a larger network.

90. **Switch:** A network device that filters and forwards packets between LAN segments.

91. **Syslog:** A protocol for message logging and event tracking in network devices.

92. **TCP (Transmission Control Protocol):** A reliable, connection-oriented transport protocol.

93. **Throughput:** The actual rate of successful data transfer over a communication channel.

94. **TKIP (Temporal Key Integrity Protocol):** A deprecated wireless encryption protocol once used with WPA.

95. **Traceroute:** A tool that shows the path a packet takes to a destination.

96. **Tunneling:** The practice of encapsulating one protocol within another.

97. **UDP (User Datagram Protocol):** A connectionless transport protocol with no delivery guarantee.

98. **Unicast:** Communication between a single sender and a single receiver over a network.

99. **Uplink:** A connection from a device to a higher-level device or network.

100. **UTM (Unified Threat Management):** A security appliance that integrates multiple security functions.

101. **VLAN (Virtual Local Area Network):** A logical segmentation of network devices.

102. **VPN (Virtual Private Network):** A secure tunnel over a public network.

103. **WAN (Wide Area Network):** A network that spans a large geographic area.

104. **WAP (Wireless Access Point):** A device that allows wireless devices to connect to a wired network.

105. **Wireshark:** A packet analyzer used for network troubleshooting and analysis.

106. **Worm:** A type of malware that replicates itself to spread to other computers.

107. **WPA2 (Wi-Fi Protected Access 2):** A security protocol used to secure wireless networks with AES encryption.

108. **Zero Trust:** A security model that assumes no trust and enforces strict access controls.

109. **Zombie Process:** A defunct process that remains in a system's process table after completion.

Index

351

K. A. Cochran, *CompTIA Network+ (N10-009) Certification Companion*,
Certification Study Companion Series, https://doi.org/10.1007/979-8-8688-2341-1

D

E

L

M

Monitoring method (*cont.*)
    syslog, 67
    throughput, 70
    visualization and reporting, 71
Monitoring system
    align polling intervals, 218
    baselines, 222
    layered monitoring, 220
    logging/alerting
        system, 224–227
    logging protocol, 216
    Nagios/Zabbix/PRTG, 219
    NetFlow/sFlow/IPFIX, 217
    Nmap, 219
    performance metrics, 221–223
    ping/traceroute, 219
    protocols, 216–218
    reachability tests, 215
    references, 228
    secure access, 220
    secure versions, 217
    SIEM platforms, 219
    SolarWinds/ManageEngine, 219
    syslog, 217
    tools, 218–220
    tune alerts, 220
    wireshark, 219
Multi-factor authentication (MFA),
    91, 197, 253
Multiple Input, Multiple Output
    (MIMO), 145
Multi-User MIMO
    (MU-MIMO), 146

N

Network access control (NAC),
    186, 270
Networking technology
    cloud deployment, 41–44
    components, 14
        access points (APs), 15
        connectors/cables, 15
        host-based firewall, 15
        modems, 15
        nodes, 14
        routers, 15
        switches, 14, 16 (*see also*
        Computer networking)
    devices, 37–39
        access point (AP), 38
        firewall, 39
        hub/switch, 37
        modem, 38
        modulation/
        demodulation, 39
        router, 38
    foundational core, 13
    IP addressing, 20–23
    models, 16
    OSI model, 17–18
    protocols/ports, 19–20
    structured cabling
        systems, 39–40
    TCP/IP model, 18–19
    topologies, 35–37
    types, 26

S

GPSR Compliance
The European Union's (EU) General Product Safety Regulation (GPSR) is a set
of rules that requires consumer products to be safe and our obligations to
ensure this.

If you have any concerns about our products, you can contact us on

ProductSafety@springernature.com

In case Publisher is established outside the EU, the EU authorized
representative is:

Springer Nature Customer Service Center GmbH
Europaplatz 3
69115 Heidelberg, Germany